RECIPES FOR
MEAT LOVERS

Publications International, Ltd.

TABLE of CONTENTS

SLOW COOKING 101

SIZES OF CROCK-POT® SLOW COOKERS

Smaller **CROCK-POT®** slow cookers— such as 1- to 3½-quart models—are the perfect size for cooking for singles, a couple, or empty nesters (and also for serving dips).

While medium-size **CROCK-POT®** slow cookers (those holding somewhere between 3 quarts and 5 quarts) will easily cook enough food at one time to feed a small family. They are also convenient for holiday side dishes or appetizers.

Large **CROCK-POT®** slow cookers are great for large family dinners, holiday entertaining, and potluck suppers. A 6- to 7-quart model is ideal if you like to make meals in advance. Or, have dinner tonight and store leftovers for later.

TYPES OF CROCK-POT® SLOW COOKERS

Current **CROCK-POT®** slow cookers come equipped with many different features and benefits, from auto cook programs to oven-safe stoneware to timed programming. Please visit **WWW.CROCK-POT.COM** to find the **CROCK-POT®** slow cooker that best suits your needs.

How you plan to use a **CROCK-POT®** slow cooker may affect the model you choose to purchase. For everyday cooking, choose a size large enough to serve your family. If you plan to use the **CROCK-POT®** slow cooker primarily for entertaining, choose one of the larger sizes. Basic **CROCK-POT®** slow cookers can hold as little as 16 ounces or as much as 7 quarts. The smallest sizes are great for keeping dips warm on a buffet, while the larger sizes can more readily fit large quantities of food and larger roasts.

COOKING, STIRRING, AND FOOD SAFETY

CROCK-POT® slow cookers are safe to leave unattended. The outer heating base may get hot as it cooks, but it should not pose a fire hazard. The heating element in the heating base functions at a low wattage and is safe for your countertops.

Your **CROCK-POT**® slow cooker should be filled about one-half to three-fourths full for most recipes unless otherwise instructed. Lean meats such as chicken or pork tenderloin will cook faster than meats with more connective tissue and fat such as beef chuck or pork shoulder. Bone-in meats will take longer than boneless cuts. Typical **CROCK-POT**® slow cooker dishes take approximately 7 to 8 hours to reach the simmer point on LOW and about 3 to 4 hours on HIGH. Once the vegetables and meat start to simmer and braise, their flavors will fully blend and meat will become fall-off-the-bone tender.

According to the U.S. Department of Agriculture, all bacteria are killed at a temperature of 165°F. It's important to follow the recommended cooking times and not to open the lid often, especially early in the cooking process when heat is building up inside the unit. If you need to open the lid to check on your food or are adding additional ingredients, remember to allow additional cooking time if necessary to ensure food is cooked through and tender.

Large **CROCK-POT**® slow cookers, the 6- to 7-quart sizes, may benefit from a quick stir halfway through cook time to help distribute heat and promote even cooking. It's usually unnecessary to stir at all, as even ½ cup liquid will help to distribute heat and the stoneware is the perfect medium for holding food at an even temperature throughout the cooking process.

OVEN-SAFE STONEWARE

All **CROCK-POT**® slow cooker removable stoneware inserts may (without their lids) be used safely in ovens at up to 400°F. In addition, all **CROCK-POT**® slow cookers are microwavable without their lids. If you own another slow cooker brand, please refer to your owner's manual for specific stoneware cooking medium tolerances.

FROZEN FOOD

Frozen food can be successfully cooked in a **CROCK-POT**® slow cooker. However, it will require additional cooking time than the same recipe made with fresh food. It is preferable to thaw frozen food prior to placing it in the **CROCK-POT**® slow cooker. Using an instant-read thermometer is recommended to ensure meat is fully cooked through.

PASTA AND RICE

To convert a recipe for a **CROCK-POT®** slow cooker that calls for uncooked pasta, first cook the pasta on the stovetop just until slightly tender. Then add the pasta to the **CROCK-POT®** slow cooker. If you are converting a recipe for the **CROCK-POT®** slow cooker that calls for cooked rice, stir in raw rice with the other recipe ingredients plus ¼ cup extra liquid per ¼ cup of raw rice.

BEANS

Beans must be softened completely before combining with sugar and/or acidic foods in the **CROCK-POT®** slow cooker. Sugar and acid have a hardening effect on beans and will prevent softening. Fully cooked canned beans may be used as a substitute for dried beans.

VEGETABLES

Root vegetables often cook more slowly than meat. Cut vegetables accordingly to cook at the same rate as meat—large versus small or lean versus marbled—and place near the sides or bottom of the stoneware to facilitate cooking.

HERBS

Fresh herbs add flavor and color when added at the end of the cooking cycle; if added at the beginning, many fresh herbs' flavor will dissipate over long cook times. Ground and/or dried herbs and spices work well in slow cooking and may be added at the beginning of cook time. For dishes with shorter cook times, hearty fresh herbs such as rosemary and thyme hold up well. The flavor power of all herbs and spices can vary greatly depending on their particular strength and shelf life. Use chili powders and garlic powder sparingly, as these can sometimes intensify over the long cook times. Always taste the finished dish and correct seasonings including salt and pepper.

LIQUIDS

It's not necessary to use more than ½ to 1 cup liquid in most instances since juices in meats and vegetables are retained more in slow cooking than in conventional cooking. Excess liquid can be cooked down and concentrated after slow cooking on the stovetop or by removing meat and vegetables from the stoneware, stirring in one of the following thickeners, and setting the **CROCK-POT®** slow cooker to HIGH. Cover; cook on HIGH for approximately 15 minutes or until juices are thickened.

FLOUR: All-purpose flour is often used to thicken soups or stews. Stir water into the flour in a small bowl until smooth. With the **CROCK-POT®** slow cooker on HIGH, whisk flour mixture into the liquid in the **CROCK-POT®** slow cooker. Cover; cook on HIGH 15 minutes or until the mixture is thickened.

CORNSTARCH: Cornstarch gives sauces a clear, shiny appearance; it's used most often for sweet dessert sauces and stir-fry sauces. Stir water into the cornstarch in a small bowl until the cornstarch is dissolved. Quickly stir this mixture into the liquid in the **CROCK-POT®** slow cooker; the sauce will thicken as soon as the liquid simmers. Cornstarch breaks down with too much heat, so never add it at the beginning of the slow cooking process and turn off the heat as soon as the sauce is thickened.

TAPIOCA: Tapioca is a starchy substance extracted from the root of the cassava plant. Its greatest advantage is that it withstands long cooking, making it an ideal choice for slow cooking. Add tapioca at the beginning of cooking and you'll get a clear, thickened sauce in the finished dish. Dishes using tapioca as a thickener are best cooked on the LOW setting; it may become stringy when boiled for a long time.

MILK

Milk, cream, and sour cream break down during extended cooking. When possible, add them during the last 15 to 30 minutes of slow cooking, until just heated through. Condensed soups may be substituted for milk and may cook for extended times.

FISH

Fish is delicate and should be stirred into the **CROCK-POT®** slow cooker gently during the last 15 to 30 minutes of cooking. Cover; cook just until cooked through and serve immediately.

BAKED GOODS

If you wish to prepare bread, cakes, or pudding cakes in a **CROCK-POT®** slow cooker, you may want to purchase a covered, vented metal cake pan accessory for your **CROCK-POT®** slow cooker. You can also use any straight-sided soufflé dish or deep cake pan that will fit into the stoneware of your unit. Baked goods can be prepared directly in the stoneware; however, they can be a little difficult to remove from the insert, so follow the recipe directions carefully.

RIBS AND WINGS

MAPLE-DRY RUBBED RIBS

MAKES 4 SERVINGS

2 teaspoons chili powder, divided

1 teaspoon ground coriander

1 teaspoon garlic powder, divided

½ teaspoon salt

¼ teaspoon black pepper

3 to 3½ pounds pork baby back ribs, trimmed and cut in half

3 tablespoons maple syrup, divided

1 can (about 8 ounces) tomato sauce

¼ teaspoon ground cinnamon

¼ teaspoon ground ginger

1. Coat inside of **CROCK-POT**® slow cooker with nonstick cooking spray. Combine 1 teaspoon chili powder, coriander, ½ teaspoon garlic powder, salt and pepper in small bowl; stir to blend. Brush ribs with 1 tablespoon syrup; rub with spice mixture. Remove ribs to **CROCK-POT**® slow cooker.

2. Combine tomato sauce, remaining 1 teaspoon chili powder, ½ teaspoon garlic powder, 2 tablespoons syrup, cinnamon and ginger in medium bowl; stir to blend. Pour tomato sauce mixture over ribs in **CROCK-POT**® slow cooker. Cover; cook on LOW 8 to 9 hours.

3. Remove ribs to large serving platter; cover with foil to keep warm. Turn **CROCK-POT**® slow cooker to HIGH. Cover; cook on HIGH 10 to 15 minutes or until sauce is thickened. Brush ribs with sauce and serve any remaining sauce on the side.

ASIAN GINGER CHICKEN WINGS

MAKES 6 TO 8 SERVINGS

3 pounds chicken wings, tips removed and split at the joints

1 cup chopped red onion

1 cup soy sauce

¾ cup packed brown sugar

¼ cup dry sherry

2 tablespoons chopped fresh ginger

2 cloves garlic, minced

Chopped fresh chives

1. Coat inside of **CROCK-POT®** slow cooker with nonstick cooking spray. Preheat broiler. Spray large baking sheet with nonstick cooking spray. Arrange wings on prepared sheet. Broil 6 to 8 minutes until browned, turning once. Remove to **CROCK-POT®** slow cooker.

2. Combine onion, soy sauce, brown sugar, sherry, ginger and garlic in medium bowl; stir until well blended. Add to **CROCK-POT®** slow cooker; stir to coat.

3. Cover; cook on LOW 5 to 6 hours or on HIGH 2 to 3 hours. Sprinkle with chives before serving.

SAUERKRAUT PORK RIBS

MAKES 12 SERVINGS

1 tablespoon vegetable oil

3 to 4 pounds pork country-style ribs

1 large onion, thinly sliced

1 teaspoon caraway seeds

½ teaspoon garlic powder

¼ to ½ teaspoon black pepper

¾ cup water

2 jars (about 28 ounces *each*) sauerkraut

12 medium red potatoes, quartered

1. Heat oil in large skillet over medium-low heat. Brown ribs on all sides. Remove to **CROCK-POT**® slow cooker using slotted spoon. Drain fat from skillet.

2. Add onion to skillet; cook until tender. Add caraway seeds, garlic powder and pepper; cook 15 minutes. Remove onion mixture to **CROCK-POT**® slow cooker.

3. Add water to skillet, stirring to scrape up brown bits. Pour pan juices into **CROCK-POT**® slow cooker. Partially drain sauerkraut; pour over meat. Top with potatoes. Cover; cook on LOW 6 to 8 hours or until potatoes are tender, stirring once during cooking.

"MELT YOUR MOUTH" DRUMMETTES

MAKES 8 SERVINGS

4 pounds chicken wing drummettes

2 teaspoons creole seasoning

1/8 teaspoon black pepper

2½ cups hot pepper sauce

¼ cup vegetable oil

¼ cup vinegar

4 teaspoons honey

1 teaspoon red pepper flakes

1 cup blue cheese dressing

Fresh celery stalks

1. Preheat broiler. Place drummettes on rack in broiler pan; season with creole seasoning and black pepper. Broil 4 to 5 inches from heat 10 to 12 minutes or until browned, turning once. Remove wings to **CROCK-POT**® slow cooker using slotted spoon.

2. Combine hot pepper sauce, oil, vinegar, honey and red pepper flakes in medium bowl; stir to blend. Pour over drummettes. Cover; cook on LOW 5 to 6 hours. Serve with dressing and celery.

ITALIAN BRAISED SHORT RIBS IN RED WINE

MAKES 4 TO 6 SERVINGS

3 pounds beef short ribs, trimmed

Salt and black pepper

1 tablespoon vegetable oil, plus additional as needed

2 onions, sliced

2 packages (8 ounces *each*) cremini mushrooms, quartered

2 cups dry red wine

2 cups beef broth

2 teaspoons Italian seasoning

2 cloves garlic, minced

Mashed potatoes (optional)

1. Coat inside of **CROCK-POT**® slow cooker with nonstick cooking spray. Season short ribs with salt and pepper. Heat 1 tablespoon oil in large skillet over medium-high heat. Working in batches, brown ribs on all sides, adding additional oil as needed. Remove to **CROCK-POT**® slow cooker.

2. Return skillet to heat. Add onions; cook and stir 3 minutes or until translucent. Stir in mushrooms, wine, broth, Italian seasoning and garlic; bring to a simmer. Simmer 3 minutes; pour over short ribs.

3. Cover; cook on LOW 10 to 12 hours or on HIGH 6 to 8 hours. Season with salt and pepper. Remove ribs and mushrooms to large serving platter. Strain cooking liquid; serve with cooking liquid and mashed potatoes, if desired.

MOROCCAN-SPICED CHICKEN WINGS

MAKES 8 TO 10 SERVINGS

1 tablespoon olive oil

5 pounds chicken wings, tips removed and split at joints

¼ cup orange juice

3 tablespoons tomato paste

2 teaspoons ground cumin

1 teaspoon salt

1 teaspoon curry powder

1 teaspoon ground turmeric

½ teaspoon ground ginger

½ teaspoon ground cinnamon

1. Heat oil in large skillet over medium-high heat. Add wings in batches; cook 6 minutes or until browned on all sides. Remove wings to **CROCK-POT**® slow cooker using slotted spoon.

2. Combine orange juice, tomato paste, cumin, salt, curry powder, turmeric, ginger and cinnamon in large bowl; stir to blend. Pour over wings. Cover; cook on LOW 6 to 7 hours or on HIGH 3 to 3½ hours.

MANGO SPICED RIBS

MAKES 6 SERVINGS

2 tablespoons vegetable oil

3 pounds beef short ribs

1 cup mango chutney

1 teaspoon curry powder

1 clove garlic, minced

½ teaspoon salt

½ teaspoon ground cinnamon

1. Heat oil in large skillet over medium heat. Add ribs; cook 3 to 5 minutes or until browned on all sides.

2. Combine chutney, curry powder, garlic, salt and cinnamon in medium bowl; rub mixture onto ribs. Place in **CROCK-POT**® slow cooker. Drizzle remaining chutney mixture over ribs. Cover; cook on LOW 6 to 8 hours or on HIGH 3 to 4 hours.

SALSA-STYLE WINGS

MAKES 4 SERVINGS

2 tablespoons
   vegetable oil

1½ pounds chicken
   wings (about
   18 wings)

2 cups salsa

¼ cup packed brown
   sugar

   Sprigs fresh cilantro
   (optional)

1. Heat oil in large skillet over medium-high heat. Add wings in batches; cook 3 to 4 minutes or until browned on all sides. Remove to **CROCK-POT**® slow cooker.

2. Combine salsa and brown sugar in medium bowl; stir to blend. Pour over wings. Cover; cook on LOW 5 to 6 hours or on HIGH 2 to 3 hours. Serve with salsa mixture. Garnish with cilantro.

SOY-BRAISED CHICKEN WINGS

MAKES 2 DOZEN WINGS

¼ cup dry sherry

¼ cup soy sauce

3 tablespoons sugar

2 tablespoons cornstarch

2 tablespoons minced garlic, divided

2 teaspoons red pepper flakes

2½ pounds chicken wings, tips removed and split at joints

2 tablespoons vegetable oil

3 green onions, cut into 1-inch pieces

¼ cup chicken broth

1 teaspoon sesame oil

1 tablespoon sesame seeds, toasted*

*To toast sesame seeds, spread in small skillet. Shake skillet over medium heat 3 minutes or until seeds begin to pop and turn golden brown.

1. Combine sherry, soy sauce, sugar, cornstarch, 1 tablespoon garlic and red pepper flakes in large bowl; stir to blend. Reserve ¼ cup marinade in separate small bowl. Stir wings into remaining marinade. Cover; marinate in refrigerator overnight.

2. Drain wings; discard marinade. Heat vegetable oil in large skillet over high heat. Add wings in batches; cook 3 to 4 minutes or until browned on all sides. Remove to **CROCK-POT**® slow cooker using slotted spoon.

3. Add remaining 1 tablespoon garlic and green onions to skillet; cook and stir 30 seconds. Stir in broth; pour over wings.

4. Cover; cook on HIGH 2 hours. Remove wings to large serving platter. Add sesame oil to reserved marinade; stir to blend. Pour over wings; sprinkle with sesame seeds.

SWEET GINGERED SPARERIBS

MAKES 4 TO 6 SERVINGS

4 to 6 pounds pork spareribs, cut into 1- or 2-rib portions

Salt and black pepper

½ cup soy sauce

⅓ cup honey

¼ cup dry sherry

1 clove garlic, minced

¼ to ½ teaspoon ground ginger

2 tablespoons water

1 tablespoon cornstarch

1. Heat large skillet over medium-high heat. Season ribs with salt and pepper. Add ribs in batches; cook 3 to 5 minutes or until browned on both sides. Remove to **CROCK-POT®** slow cooker.

2. Combine soy sauce, honey, sherry, garlic and ginger in small bowl; pour over ribs. Cover; cook on LOW 6 to 8 hours.

3. Turn **CROCK-POT®** slow cooker to HIGH. Remove ribs to large serving platter. Stir water into cornstarch in small bowl until smooth. Whisk into **CROCK-POT®** slow cooker. Cook, uncovered, on HIGH 5 to 10 minutes or until sauce begins to thicken. Return ribs to thickened sauce; stir to coat.

HOISIN SRIRACHA CHICKEN WINGS

MAKES 5 TO 6 SERVINGS

3 pounds chicken wings, tips removed and split at joints

½ cup hoisin sauce

¼ cup plus 1 tablespoon sriracha sauce, divided

2 tablespoons packed brown sugar

Chopped green onions (optional)

1. Coat inside of **CROCK-POT®** slow cooker with nonstick cooking spray. Preheat broiler. Spray large baking sheet with nonstick cooking spray. Arrange wings on prepared baking sheet. Broil 6 to 8 minutes or until browned, turning once. Remove wings to **CROCK-POT®** slow cooker.

2. Combine hoisin sauce, ¼ cup sriracha sauce and brown sugar in medium bowl; stir to blend. Pour sauce mixture over wings in **CROCK-POT®** slow cooker; stir to coat. Cover; cook on LOW 3½ to 4 hours. Remove wings to large serving platter; cover with foil to keep warm.

3. Turn **CROCK-POT®** slow cooker to HIGH. Cook, uncovered, on HIGH 10 to 15 minutes or until sauce is thickened. Stir in remaining 1 tablespoon sriracha sauce. Spoon sauce over wings to serve. Garnish with green onions.

HEARTY BABY BACK PORK RIBS

MAKES 6 TO 8 SERVINGS

2½ pounds pork baby back ribs, trimmed and cut into 2-rib portions

1 to 2 tablespoons coarse salt

1 to 2 tablespoons black pepper

2 tablespoons olive oil, divided

2 carrots, diced

2 stalks celery, diced

1 large yellow onion, diced

3 cloves garlic, minced

3 whole bay leaves

⅓ cup dry red wine

⅓ cup crushed tomatoes

⅓ cup balsamic vinegar

Carrot slices, cooked (optional)

Hot cooked noodles (optional)

1. Season ribs with salt and pepper. Drizzle with 1 tablespoon oil. Heat remaining 1 tablespoon oil in large skillet. Cook ribs 2 to 3 minutes per side or until just browned. Remove ribs to **CROCK-POT®** slow cooker. Add diced carrots, celery, onion, garlic and bay leaves.

2. Combine wine, tomatoes and vinegar in small bowl. Season with salt and pepper, if desired. Pour mixture into **CROCK-POT®** slow cooker. Cover; cook on LOW 8 to 9 hours or on HIGH 5 to 6 hours, turning once or twice, until meat is tender and falling off the bone.

3. Remove ribs to large serving platter. Remove and discard bay leaves. Add sauce to food processor or blender; process to desired consistency. Pour sauce over ribs. Serve with sliced carrots and noodles, if desired.

RASPBERRY BBQ CHICKEN WINGS

MAKES 5 TO 6 SERVINGS

3 pounds (10 to 12) chicken wings, tips removed and split at joints

¾ cup seedless raspberry jam

½ cup sweet and tangy prepared barbecue sauce

1 tablespoon raspberry red wine vinegar

1 teaspoon chili powder

1. Coat inside of **CROCK-POT**® slow cooker with nonstick cooking spray. Preheat broiler. Spray large baking sheet with nonstick cooking spray. Arrange wings on prepared sheet. Broil 6 to 8 minutes until browned, turning once. Remove to **CROCK-POT**® slow cooker.

2. Combine jam, barbecue sauce, vinegar and chili powder in medium bowl; stir to blend. Pour sauce over wings in **CROCK-POT**® slow cooker; stir to coat. Cover; cook on LOW 3½ to 4 hours. Remove wings to large serving platter; cover to keep warm.

3. Turn **CROCK-POT**® slow cooker to HIGH. Cook, uncovered, on HIGH 10 to 15 minutes or until sauce is thickened. Spoon sauce over wings to serve.

BRAISED SHORT RIBS WITH AROMATIC SPICES

MAKES 4 SERVINGS

1 tablespoon olive oil

3 pounds bone-in beef short ribs, trimmed

1 teaspoon ground cumin, divided

1 teaspoon salt

½ teaspoon black pepper

2 medium onions, halved and thinly sliced

10 cloves garlic, thinly sliced

2 tablespoons balsamic vinegar

2 tablespoons honey

1 whole cinnamon stick

2 whole star anise pods

2 large sweet potatoes, peeled and cut into ¾-inch cubes

1 cup beef broth

1. Heat oil in large skillet over medium-high heat. Season ribs with ½ teaspoon cumin, salt and pepper. Add to skillet; cook 8 minutes or until browned, turning occasionally. Remove ribs to large plate.

2. Heat same skillet over medium heat. Add onions and garlic; cook 12 to 14 minutes or until onions are lightly browned. Stir in vinegar; cook 1 minute. Add remaining ½ teaspoon cumin, honey, cinnamon stick and star anise; cook and stir 30 seconds. Remove mixture to **CROCK-POT**® slow cooker. Stir in potatoes; top with ribs. Pour in broth.

3. Cover; cook on LOW 8 to 9 hours or until meat is falling off the bones. Remove and discard bones from ribs. Remove and discard cinnamon stick and star anise. Turn off heat. Let mixture stand 5 to 10 minutes. Skim off and discard fat. Serve meat with sauce and vegetables.

BIG BOWLS

CLASSIC CHILI
MAKES 6 SERVINGS

1½ pounds ground beef

1½ cups chopped onion

1 cup chopped green bell pepper

2 cloves garlic, minced

3 cans (about 15 ounces *each*) dark red kidney beans, rinsed and drained

2 cans (about 15 ounces *each*) tomato sauce

1 can (about 14 ounces) diced tomatoes

2 to 3 teaspoons chili powder

1 to 2 teaspoons ground mustard

¾ teaspoon dried basil

½ teaspoon black pepper

1 to 2 dried red chiles (optional)

1. Brown beef, onion, bell pepper and garlic in large skillet over medium-high heat, stirring to break up meat. Remove beef mixture to **CROCK-POT**® slow cooker using slotted spoon.

2. Add beans, tomato sauce, tomatoes, chili powder, mustard, basil, black pepper and chiles, if desired, to **CROCK-POT**® slow cooker; mix well. Cover; cook on LOW 8 to 10 hours or on HIGH 4 to 5 hours. If used, remove chiles before serving.

BEEF STEW WITH BACON, ONION AND SWEET POTATOES

MAKES 4 SERVINGS

1 pound cubed beef
   stew meat

1 can (about
   14 ounces)
   beef broth

2 medium sweet
   potatoes, cut into
   2-inch pieces

1 large onion,
   chopped

2 slices thick-cut
   bacon, diced

1 teaspoon dried
   thyme

1 teaspoon salt

¼ teaspoon black
   pepper

2 tablespoons water

2 tablespoons
   cornstarch

1. Coat inside of **CROCK-POT**® slow cooker with nonstick cooking spray. Combine beef, broth, potatoes, onion, bacon, thyme, salt and pepper in **CROCK-POT**® slow cooker; stir to blend.

2. Cover; cook on LOW 7 to 8 hours or on HIGH 4 to 5 hours. Remove beef and vegetables to large serving bowl using slotted spoon. Cover and keep warm.

3. Stir water into cornstarch in small bowl until smooth. Whisk into cooking liquid in **CROCK-POT**® slow cooker. Cover; cook on LOW 15 minutes or until thickened. Serve sauce evenly over beef and vegetables.

SCALLOPS IN FRESH TOMATO AND HERB SAUCE

MAKES 4 SERVINGS

2 tablespoons vegetable oil

1 medium red onion, peeled and diced

1 clove garlic, minced

3½ cups fresh tomatoes, peeled*

1 can (12 ounces) tomato pureé

1 can (6 ounces) tomato paste

¼ cup dry red wine

2 tablespoons chopped fresh Italian parsley

1 tablespoon chopped fresh oregano

¼ teaspoon black pepper

1½ pounds fresh scallops, cleaned and drained

Hot cooked pasta or rice (optional)

*To peel tomatoes, place one at a time in simmering water about 10 seconds. (Add 30 seconds if tomatoes are not fully ripened.) Immediately plunge into a bowl of cold water for another 10 seconds. Peel skin with a knife.

1. Heat oil in medium skillet over medium heat. Add onion and garlic; cook and stir 7 to 8 minutes or until onion is soft and translucent. Remove to **CROCK-POT®** slow cooker.

2. Add tomatoes, tomato purée, tomato paste, wine, parsley, oregano and pepper. Cover; cook on LOW 6 to 8 hours.

3. Turn **CROCK-POT®** slow cooker to HIGH. Add scallops. Cook on HIGH 15 minutes or until scallops are cooked through. Serve over pasta, if desired.

CHORIZO CHILI

MAKES 6 SERVINGS

1 pound ground beef

8 ounces bulk raw chorizo sausage *or* ½ (15-ounce) package raw chorizo sausage, casings removed*

1 can (about 15 ounces) chili beans in chili sauce

2 cans (about 14 ounces *each*) chili-style diced tomatoes

Optional toppings: sour cream, chives and shredded Cheddar cheese

*A highly seasoned Mexican pork sausage.

1. Brown beef and chorizo in large skillet over medium-high heat 6 to 8 minutes, stirring to break up meat. Remove beef mixture to **CROCK-POT**® slow cooker using slotted spoon. Stir beans and tomatoes into **CROCK-POT**® slow cooker.

2. Cover; cook on LOW 7 hours. Turn off heat. Let stand 10 to 12 minutes. Skim fat from surface. Top as desired.

BEEF FAJITA SOUP

MAKES 8 SERVINGS

1 pound cubed beef
   stew meat

1 can (about 15 ounces)
   pinto beans, rinsed
   and drained

1 can (about 15 ounces)
   black beans, rinsed
   and drained

1 can (about 14 ounces)
   diced tomatoes
   with roasted garlic

1 can (about 14 ounces)
   beef broth

1½ cups water

1 green bell pepper,
   thinly sliced

1 red bell pepper, thinly
   sliced

1 onion, thinly sliced

2 teaspoons ground
   cumin

1 teaspoon seasoned
   salt

1 teaspoon black
   pepper

   Shredded cheese
   (optional)

Combine beef, beans, tomatoes, broth, water, bell peppers, onion, cumin, salt and black pepper in **CROCK-POT**® slow cooker; stir to blend. Cover; cook on LOW 8 hours. Top with cheese, if desired.

BEEFY TORTELLINI

MAKES 6 SERVINGS

½ pound ground beef or turkey

1 jar (24 to 26 ounces) roasted tomato and garlic pasta sauce

1 package (12 ounces) uncooked three-cheese tortellini

8 ounces sliced button or exotic mushrooms, such as oyster, shiitake and cremini

½ cup water

½ teaspoon red pepper flakes (optional)

¾ cup grated Asiago or Romano cheese

Chopped fresh Italian parsley (optional)

1. Coat inside of **CROCK-POT**® slow cooker with nonstick cooking spray. Brown beef in large skillet over medium-high heat 6 to 8 minutes, stirring to break up meat. Remove to **CROCK-POT**® slow cooker using slotted spoon.

2. Stir pasta sauce, tortellini, mushrooms, water and red pepper flakes, if desired, into **CROCK-POT**® slow cooker. Cover; cook on LOW 2 hours or on HIGH 1 hour. Stir.

3. Cover; cook on LOW 2 to 2½ hours or on HIGH ½ to 1 hour. Serve in shallow bowls topped with cheese and parsley, if desired.

BEEF AND BLACK BEAN CHILI

MAKES 4 SERVINGS

1 tablespoon vegetable
   oil

1 pound boneless beef
   round steak, cut
   into 1-inch cubes

1 package (14 ounces)
   frozen green and
   red bell pepper
   strips with onions

1 can (about 15 ounces)
   black beans, rinsed
   and drained

1 can (about 14 ounces)
   fire-roasted diced
   tomatoes

2 tablespoons chili
   powder

1 tablespoon minced
   garlic

2 teaspoons ground
   cumin

½ ounce semisweet
   chocolate,
   chopped

Hot cooked rice

Shredded Cheddar
   cheese (optional)

Prepared corn bread
   (optional)

1. Heat oil in large skillet over medium-high heat. Brown beef on all sides. Remove to **CROCK-POT®** slow cooker using slotted spoon.

2. Stir pepper strips with onions, beans, tomatoes, chili powder, garlic and cumin into **CROCK-POT®** slow cooker. Cover; cook on LOW 8 to 9 hours. Turn off heat; stir in chocolate until melted. Serve over rice; garnish with cheese. Serve with corn bread, if desired.

MEXICAN CHICKEN AND BLACK BEAN SOUP

MAKES 4 SERVINGS

4 bone-in chicken thighs, skin removed

1 can (about 14 ounces) chicken broth

1 can (about 14 ounces) diced tomatoes with Mexican seasoning or diced tomatoes with mild green chiles

1 can (about 15 ounces) black beans, rinsed and drained

1 cup chopped onion

1 cup frozen corn

1 can (4 ounces) chopped mild green chiles

1 tablespoon chili powder

1 teaspoon salt

1 teaspoon ground cumin

Fried tortilla strips (optional)

1. Coat inside of **CROCK-POT**® slow cooker with nonstick cooking spray. Add chicken, broth, tomatoes, beans, onion, corn, chiles, chili powder, salt and cumin; stir to blend. Cover; cook on HIGH 3 to 4 hours.

2. Remove chicken to large cutting board with slotted spoon. Debone and chop chicken. Return to **CROCK-POT**® slow cooker; stir to blend. Top with tortilla strips, if desired.

PIZZA-STYLE MOSTACCIOLI

MAKES 4 SERVINGS

1 jar (24 to 26 ounces) marinara sauce or tomato basil pasta sauce

½ cup water

1 package (8 ounces) sliced mushrooms

1 small yellow or green bell pepper, finely diced

½ cup (1 ounce) sliced pepperoni, halved

1 teaspoon dried oregano

¼ teaspoon red pepper flakes

2 cups (6 ounces) uncooked mostaccioli pasta

1 cup (4 ounces) shredded pizza cheese blend or Italian cheese blend

Chopped fresh oregano (optional)

Garlic bread (optional)

1. Coat inside of **CROCK-POT**® slow cooker with nonstick cooking spray. Combine marinara sauce and water in **CROCK-POT**® slow cooker. Stir in mushrooms, bell pepper, pepperoni, dried oregano and red pepper flakes; mix well. Cover; cook on LOW 2 hours or on HIGH 1 hour.

2. Stir in pasta. Cover; cook on LOW 1½ to 2 hours or on HIGH 45 minutes to 1 hour or until pasta and vegetables are tender. Spoon into shallow bowls. Top with cheese and garnish with fresh oregano. Serve with bread, if desired.

TIP: *To prevent the pasta from becoming overcooked on the bottom of the **CROCK-POT**® slow cooker, stir it halfway through cooking time.*

CLASSIC BEEF STEW

MAKES 8 SERVINGS

2½ pounds cubed beef stew meat

¼ cup all-purpose flour

2 tablespoons olive oil, divided

3 cups beef broth

16 baby carrots

8 fingerling potatoes, halved crosswise

1 medium onion, chopped

1 ounce dried oyster mushrooms, chopped

2 teaspoons garlic powder

1 teaspoon dried basil

1 teaspoon dried oregano

½ teaspoon dried rosemary

½ teaspoon dried marjoram

½ teaspoon dried sage

½ teaspoon dried thyme

Salt and black pepper (optional)

Fresh chopped Italian parsley (optional)

1. Combine beef and flour in large bowl; toss well to coat. Heat 1 tablespoon oil in large skillet over medium-high heat. Add half of beef; cook and stir 4 minutes or until browned. Remove to **CROCK-POT®** slow cooker. Repeat with remaining oil and beef.

2. Add broth, carrots, potatoes, onion, mushrooms, garlic powder, basil, oregano, rosemary, marjoram, sage and thyme to **CROCK-POT®** slow cooker; stir to blend. Cover; cook on LOW 10 to 12 hours or on HIGH 5 to 6 hours. Season with salt and pepper, if desired. Garnish with parsley.

WEEKNIGHT CHILI

MAKES 4 SERVINGS

1 pound ground beef or turkey

1 package (about 1 ounce) chili seasoning mix

1 can (about 15 ounces) red kidney beans, rinsed and drained

1 can (about 14 ounces) diced tomatoes with mild green chiles

1 can (8 ounces) tomato sauce

1 cup (4 ounces) shredded Cheddar cheese (optional)

Chopped green onion (optional)

1. Brown beef in large skillet over medium-high heat 6 to 8 minutes, stirring to break up meat. Drain fat. Stir in seasoning mix.

2. Combine beef mixture, beans, tomatoes and tomato sauce in **CROCK-POT®** slow cooker; stir to blend. Cover; cook on LOW 4 to 6 hours or on HIGH 2 to 3 hours. Top with cheese and green onion, if desired.

CHICKEN AND MUSHROOM STEW

MAKES 6 SERVINGS

4 tablespoons vegetable oil, divided

2 medium leeks (white and light green parts only), halved lengthwise and thinly sliced crosswise

1 carrot, cut into 1-inch pieces

1 stalk celery, diced

6 boneless, skinless chicken thighs (about 2 pounds)

Salt and black pepper

12 ounces cremini mushrooms, quartered

1 ounce dried porcini mushrooms, rehydrated in 1½ cups hot water and chopped, soaking liquid strained and reserved

1 teaspoon minced garlic

1 sprig fresh thyme

1 whole bay leaf

¼ cup all-purpose flour

½ cup dry white wine

1 cup chicken broth

1. Heat 1 tablespoon oil in large skillet over medium heat. Add leeks; cook 8 minutes or until softened. Remove to **CROCK-POT**® slow cooker. Add carrot and celery.

2. Heat 1 tablespoon oil in same skillet over medium-high heat. Season chicken with salt and pepper. Add chicken in batches; cook 8 minutes or until browned on both sides. Remove to **CROCK-POT**® slow cooker.

3. Heat remaining 2 tablespoons oil in same skillet. Add cremini mushrooms; cook 7 minutes or until mushrooms have released their liquid and started to brown. Add porcini mushrooms, garlic, thyme, bay leaf and flour; cook and stir 1 minute. Add wine; cook and stir until evaporated, stirring to scrape any browned bits from bottom of skillet. Add reserved soaking liquid and broth; bring to a simmer. Pour mixture into **CROCK-POT**® slow cooker.

4. Cover; cook on HIGH 2 to 3 hours. Remove thyme sprig and bay leaf before serving.

POZOLE ROJO

MAKES 8 SERVINGS

4 dried ancho chiles, stemmed and seeded

3 dried guajillo chiles, stemmed and seeded*

2 cups boiling water

2½ pounds boneless pork shoulder, trimmed and cut in half

3 teaspoons salt, divided

1 tablespoon vegetable oil

2 medium onions, chopped

1½ tablespoons minced garlic

2 teaspoons ground cumin

2 teaspoons Mexican oregano**

4 cups chicken broth

2 cans (30 ounces *each*) white hominy, rinsed and drained

Sliced radishes (optional)

*Guajillo chiles can be found in the ethnic section of large supermarkets.

**Mexican oregano has a stronger flavor than regular oregano. It can be found in the spices and seasonings section of most large supermarkets.

1. Place ancho and guajillo chiles in medium bowl; pour boiling water over top. Weigh down chiles with small plate or bowl; soak 30 minutes.

2. Meanwhile, season pork with 1 teaspoon salt. Heat oil in large skillet over medium-high heat. Add pork; cook 8 to 10 minutes or until browned on all sides. Remove to **CROCK-POT®** slow cooker.

3. Heat same skillet over medium heat. Add onions; cook 6 minutes or until softened. Add garlic, cumin, oregano and remaining 2 teaspoons salt; cook and stir 1 minute. Stir in broth; bring to a simmer, scraping up any browned bits from bottom of skillet. Pour over pork in **CROCK-POT®** slow cooker.

4. Place softened chiles and soaking liquid in food processor or blender; blend until smooth. Pour through fine-mesh sieve into medium bowl, pressing with spoon to extract liquid. Discard solids. Stir mixture into **CROCK-POT®** slow cooker.

5. Cover; cook on LOW 5 hours. Stir in hominy. Cover; cook on LOW 1 hour. Turn off heat. Let stand 10 to 15 minutes. Skim off fat and discard. Remove pork to large cutting board; shred with two forks. Ladle hominy mixture into bowls; top each serving with pork and radishes, if desired.

TEXAS CHILI

MAKES 8 SERVINGS

3½ to 4 pounds cubed beef stew meat

Salt and black pepper

4 tablespoons vegetable oil, divided

1 large onion, chopped

¼ cup chili powder

1 tablespoon minced garlic

1 tablespoon tomato paste

1 tablespoon ground cumin

2 teaspoons ground coriander

1 teaspoon dried oregano

3 cans (about 14 ounces *each*) diced tomatoes

3 tablespoons cornmeal or masa harina

1 tablespoon packed light brown sugar

1. Season beef with salt and pepper. Heat 3 tablespoons oil in large skillet over medium-high heat. Cook beef in batches 8 minutes or until browned on all sides. Remove to **CROCK-POT**® slow cooker using slotted spoon.

2. Heat remaining 1 tablespoon oil in same skillet. Add onion; cook and stir 6 minutes or until softened. Stir in chili powder, garlic, tomato paste, cumin, coriander, oregano, additional salt and pepper as desired; cook and stir 1 minute. Stir in tomatoes, cornmeal and brown sugar; bring to a simmer. Remove to **CROCK-POT**® slow cooker. Cover; cook on LOW 7 to 8 hours.

VARIATION: Add ¼ teaspoon ground red pepper if a spicier chili is desired.

BEEF AND BEET BORSCHT

MAKES 6 TO 8 SERVINGS

6 slices bacon

1 boneless beef chuck roast (1½ pounds), trimmed and cut into ½-inch pieces

1 medium onion, chopped

4 cloves garlic, minced

4 medium beets, peeled and cut into ½-inch pieces

2 large carrots, sliced

3 cups beef broth

6 sprigs fresh dill

3 tablespoons honey

3 tablespoons red wine vinegar

2 whole bay leaves

3 cups shredded green cabbage

1. Heat large skillet over medium heat. Add bacon; cook and stir until crisp. Remove to paper towel-lined plate using slotted spoon; crumble.

2. Return skillet to medium-high heat. Add beef; cook 5 minutes or until browned. Remove beef to **CROCK-POT®** slow cooker.

3. Pour off all but 1 tablespoon fat from skillet. Add onion and garlic; cook 4 minutes or until onion is softened. Remove onion mixture to **CROCK-POT®** slow cooker. Stir in bacon, beets, carrots, broth, dill, honey, vinegar and bay leaves.

4. Cover; cook on LOW 5 to 6 hours. Stir in cabbage. Cover; cook on LOW 30 minutes. Remove and discard bay leaves before serving.

MANLY MEALS

BONELESS PORK ROAST WITH GARLIC

MAKES 4 TO 6 SERVINGS

1 boneless pork rib roast (2 to 2½ pounds)

Salt and black pepper

3 tablespoons olive oil, divided

4 cloves garlic, minced

¼ cup chopped fresh rosemary

½ lemon, cut into ⅛- to ¼-inch slices

½ cup chicken broth

¼ cup dry white wine

1. Season pork with salt and pepper. Combine 2 tablespoons oil, garlic and rosemary in small bowl. Rub over pork. Roll and tie pork with kitchen string. Tuck lemon slices under string and into ends of roast.

2. Heat remaining 1 tablespoon oil in skillet over medium heat. Add pork; cook 6 to 8 minutes or until browned on all sides. Remove to **CROCK-POT**® slow cooker.

3. Return skillet to heat. Add broth and wine, scraping up any browned bits from bottom of skillet. Pour over pork in **CROCK-POT**® slow cooker. Cover; cook on LOW 8 to 9 hours or on HIGH 3½ to 4 hours.

4. Remove roast to large cutting board. Cover loosely with foil; let stand 10 to 15 minutes before removing kitchen string and slicing. Pour liquid from **CROCK-POT**® slow cooker over sliced pork to serve.

EASY PARMESAN CHICKEN

MAKES 4 SERVINGS

8 ounces mushrooms, sliced

1 medium onion, cut into thin wedges

1 tablespoon olive oil

4 boneless, skinless chicken breasts

1 jar (24 to 26 ounces) pasta sauce

½ teaspoon dried basil

¼ teaspoon dried oregano

1 whole bay leaf

½ cup (2 ounces) shredded mozzarella cheese

¼ cup grated Parmesan cheese

Hot cooked spaghetti

Chopped fresh basil (optional)

1. Place mushrooms and onion in **CROCK-POT**® slow cooker.

2. Heat oil in large skillet over medium-high heat. Add chicken; cook 5 to 6 minutes on each side or until browned. Place chicken in **CROCK-POT**® slow cooker. Pour pasta sauce over chicken; add dried basil, oregano and bay leaf. Cover; cook on LOW 6 to 7 hours or on HIGH 3 to 4 hours. Remove and discard bay leaf.

3. Sprinkle chicken with cheeses. Cook, uncovered, on LOW 10 minutes or until cheese is melted. Serve over spaghetti and garnish with fresh basil.

TIP: *Dairy products should be added at the end of the cooking time, because they will curdle if cooked in the* **CROCK-POT**® *slow cooker for too long.*

HARVEST HAM SUPPER

MAKES 6 SERVINGS

6 carrots, cut into
  2-inch pieces

3 medium sweet
  potatoes,
  quartered

1 to 1½ pounds
  boneless ham

1 cup maple syrup

Chopped fresh
  Italian parsley
  (optional)

1. Arrange carrots and potatoes in bottom of
   CROCK-POT® slow cooker.

2. Place ham on top of vegetables. Pour syrup over
   ham and vegetables. Cover; cook on LOW 6 to
   8 hours. Garnish with parsley.

BEEF AND VEAL MEAT LOAF

MAKES 6 SERVINGS

1 tablespoon olive oil

1 small onion, chopped

½ red bell pepper, chopped

3 cloves garlic, minced

1 teaspoon dried oregano

1 pound ground beef

1 pound ground veal

1 egg

3 tablespoons tomato paste

1 teaspoon salt

½ teaspoon black pepper

1. Coat inside of **CROCK-POT**® slow cooker with nonstick cooking spray. Heat oil in large skillet over medium-high heat. Add onion, bell pepper, garlic and oregano; cook and stir 5 minutes or until vegetables are softened. Remove onion mixture to large bowl; cool 6 minutes.

2. Add beef, veal, egg, tomato paste, salt and black pepper; mix well. Form into 9×5-inch loaf; place in **CROCK-POT**® slow cooker. Cover; cook on LOW 5 to 6 hours. Remove meat loaf to large cutting board; let stand 10 minutes before slicing.

INDIAN-STYLE APRICOT CHICKEN

MAKES 4 TO 6 SERVINGS

6 skinless chicken thighs (about 2 pounds)

¼ teaspoon salt, plus additional for seasoning

¼ teaspoon black pepper, plus additional for seasoning

1 tablespoon vegetable oil

1 large onion, chopped

2 cloves garlic, minced

2 tablespoons grated fresh ginger

½ teaspoon ground cinnamon

⅛ teaspoon ground allspice

1 can (about 14 ounces) diced tomatoes

1 cup chicken broth

1 package (8 ounces) dried apricots

Pinch saffron threads (optional)

Hot cooked basmati rice

2 tablespoons chopped fresh Italian parsley (optional)

1. Coat inside of **CROCK-POT®** slow cooker with nonstick cooking spray. Season chicken with ¼ teaspoon salt and ¼ teaspoon pepper. Heat oil in large skillet over medium-high heat. Brown chicken on all sides. Remove to **CROCK-POT®** slow cooker.

2. Add onion to skillet; cook and stir 3 to 5 minutes or until translucent. Stir in garlic, ginger, cinnamon and allspice; cook and stir 15 to 30 seconds or until mixture is fragrant. Add tomatoes and broth; cook 2 to 3 minutes or until mixture is heated through. Pour into **CROCK-POT®** slow cooker.

3. Add apricots and saffron, if desired. Cover; cook on LOW 5 to 6 hours or on HIGH 3 to 4 hours or until chicken is tender. Season additional with salt and pepper, if desired. Serve with rice and garnish with parsley.

NOTE: *To skin chicken easily, grasp skin with paper towel and pull away. Repeat with a fresh paper towel for each piece of chicken, discarding skins and towels.*

MAPLE WHISKEY-GLAZED BEEF BRISKET

MAKES 4 TO 6 SERVINGS

1 teaspoon ground red pepper

1 tablespoon coarse salt

½ teaspoon black pepper

1½ to 2 pounds beef brisket, scored with a knife on both sides

2 tablespoons olive oil

½ cup maple syrup

¼ cup whiskey

2 tablespoons packed brown sugar

1 tablespoon tomato paste

Juice of 1 orange

2 cloves garlic, crushed

4 slices (1⁄16-inch-thick *each*) fresh ginger

4 slices (½×1½-inch *each*) orange peel

Roasted Brussels sprouts (optional)

Spinach salad (optional)

1. Combine ground red pepper, salt and black pepper in small bowl; stir to blend. Rub over brisket. Place brisket in large resealable food storage bag. Set aside.

2. Combine oil, syrup, whiskey, brown sugar, tomato paste, orange juice, garlic, ginger and orange peel in small bowl; stir to blend. Pour mixture over brisket in resealable food storage bag. Refrigerate brisket 2 hours or overnight.

3. Transfer brisket and marinade to **CROCK-POT®** slow cooker. Cover, cook on LOW 7 to 9 hours, turning brisket once or twice. Adjust seasonings to taste. Slice thinly across the grain to serve. Serve with Brussels sprouts and salad, if desired.

MEATBALLS AND SPAGHETTI SAUCE

MAKES 6 TO 8 SERVINGS

2 pounds ground beef

1 cup bread crumbs

1 onion, chopped

2 eggs, beaten

¼ cup minced fresh Italian parsley

4 teaspoons minced garlic, divided

½ teaspoon dry mustard

1 teaspoon black pepper, divided

3 tablespoons olive oil, divided

1 can (28 ounces) peeled whole tomatoes

½ cup chopped fresh basil

1 teaspoon sugar

Salt

Hot cooked spaghetti

1. Combine beef, bread crumbs, onion, eggs, parsley, 2 teaspoons garlic, dry mustard and ½ teaspoon black pepper in large bowl. Form into walnut-sized balls. Heat 1 tablespoon oil in large skillet over medium heat. Brown meatballs on all sides. Remove to **CROCK-POT®** slow cooker using slotted spoon.

2. Combine tomatoes, basil, remaining 2 tablespoons oil, remaining 2 teaspoons garlic, sugar and remaining ½ teaspoon black pepper in medium bowl. Season with salt; stir to blend. Pour over meatballs, stirring to coat. Cover; cook on LOW 3 to 5 hours or on HIGH 2 to 4 hours.

3. Adjust seasonings, if desired. Serve over spaghetti.

TIP: *Recipe can be doubled for a 5-, 6- or 7-quart* **CROCK-POT®** *slow cooker.*

BASQUE CHICKEN WITH PEPPERS

MAKES 4 TO 6 SERVINGS

1 cut-up whole chicken (4 pounds)

2 teaspoons salt, divided

1 teaspoon black pepper, divided

1½ tablespoons olive oil

1 onion, chopped

1 medium green bell pepper, cut into strips

1 medium yellow bell pepper, cut into strips

1 medium red bell pepper, cut into strips

8 ounces small brown mushrooms, halved

1 can (about 14 ounces) stewed tomatoes

½ cup chicken broth

½ cup Rioja wine

3 ounces tomato paste

2 cloves garlic, minced

1 sprig fresh marjoram

1 teaspoon smoked paprika

4 ounces chopped prosciutto

1. Season chicken with 1 teaspoon salt and ½ teaspoon black pepper. Heat oil in large skillet over medium-high heat. Add chicken in batches; cook 6 to 8 minutes or until browned on all sides. Remove to **CROCK-POT**® slow cooker.

2. Heat same skillet over medium-low heat. Stir in onion; cook and stir 3 minutes or until softened. Add bell peppers and mushrooms; cook 3 minutes. Add tomatoes, broth, wine, tomato paste, garlic, marjoram, remaining 1 teaspoon salt, paprika and remaining ½ teaspoon black pepper to skillet; bring to a simmer. Simmer 3 to 4 minutes; pour over chicken in **CROCK-POT**® slow cooker. Cover; cook on LOW 5 to 6 hours or on HIGH 4 hours or until chicken is tender.

3. Ladle vegetables and sauce over chicken. Sprinkle with prosciutto.

ANDOUILLE AND CABBAGE CROCK

MAKES 8 SERVINGS

Nonstick cooking spray

1 pound andouille sausage, cut evenly into 3- to 4-inch pieces

1 small head cabbage, cut evenly into 8 wedges

1 medium onion, cut into ½-inch wedges

3 medium carrots, quartered lengthwise and cut into 3-inch pieces

8 new potatoes, cut in half

½ cup apple juice

1 can (about 14 ounces) chicken broth

1. Coat inside of **CROCK-POT**® slow cooker with cooking spray. Spray large skillet with cooking spray; heat over medium-high heat. Add sausage; cook and stir 6 to 8 minutes or until browned. Remove from heat.

2. Add cabbage, onion, carrots, potatoes, apple juice and broth to **CROCK-POT**® slow cooker; top with sausage. Cover; cook on HIGH 4 hours. Remove with slotted spoon to large serving bowl.

TIP: *Andouille is a spicy, smoked pork sausage. Feel free to substitute your favorite smoked sausage or kielbasa.*

BRAISED CHIPOTLE BEEF

MAKES 4 TO 6 SERVINGS

3 pounds boneless beef chuck roast, cut into 2-inch pieces

1½ teaspoons salt, plus additional for seasoning

½ teaspoon black pepper, plus additional for seasoning

3 tablespoons vegetable oil, divided

1 large onion, cut into 1-inch pieces

2 red bell peppers, cut into 1-inch pieces

3 tablespoons tomato paste

1 tablespoon minced garlic

1 tablespoon chipotle chili powder*

1 tablespoon paprika

1 tablespoon ground cumin

1 teaspoon dried oregano

1 cup beef broth

1 can (about 14 ounces) diced tomatoes, drained

*Or substitute conventional chili powder.

1. Pat beef dry with paper towels and season with salt and black pepper. Heat 2 tablespoons oil in large skillet over medium-high heat. Working in batches, cook beef in skillet, turning to brown all sides. Remove each batch to **CROCK-POT®** slow cooker as it is finished.

2. Return skillet to medium-high heat. Add remaining 1 tablespoon oil. Add onion; cook and stir just until softened. Add bell peppers; cook 2 minutes. Stir in tomato paste, garlic, chili powder, paprika, cumin, 1½ teaspoons salt, oregano and ½ teaspoon black pepper; cook and stir 1 minute. Remove to **CROCK-POT®** slow cooker.

3. Return skillet to heat; add broth. Cook, stirring to scrape up any browned bits from bottom of skillet. Pour over beef in **CROCK-POT®** slow cooker. Stir in tomatoes. Cover; cook on LOW 7 hours. Turn off heat. Let cooking liquid stand 5 minutes. Skim off and discard fat. Serve beef with cooking liquid.

MANLY MEALS

COQ AU VIN WITH LIMA BEANS

MAKES 8 TO 10 SERVINGS

4 pounds chicken thighs and drumsticks

3 slices bacon, cut into pieces

4 cups chicken broth

1 cup sliced mushrooms

1 cup sliced carrots

1 cup dry red wine

½ cup pearl onions

⅓ cup whiskey

3 to 4 cloves garlic, chopped

2 tablespoons tomato paste

1½ teaspoons herbes de Provence

2 whole bay leaves

Salt and black pepper

1 tablespoon water

2 tablespoons all-purpose flour

1 cup lima beans

Chopped fresh Italian parsley (optional)

Roasted red potatoes, quartered (optional)

1. Coat inside of **CROCK-POT®** slow cooker with nonstick cooking spray. Add chicken and bacon to **CROCK-POT®** slow cooker. Cover; cook on HIGH 45 minutes, turning chicken halfway through cooking time.

2. Turn **CROCK-POT®** slow cooker to LOW. Add broth, mushrooms, carrots, wine, onions, whiskey, garlic, tomato paste, herbes de Provence, bay leaves, salt and pepper to **CROCK-POT®** slow cooker. Stir water into flour in small bowl until smooth; whisk into **CROCK-POT®** slow cooker.

3. Cover; cook on LOW 6 hours. Add beans to **CROCK-POT®** slow cooker during last 10 minutes of cooking. Remove and discard bay leaves. Garnish with parsley. Serve with potatoes, if desired.

DELICIOUS PEPPER STEAK

MAKES 6 SERVINGS

2 tablespoons toasted sesame oil

2 pounds beef round steak, cut into strips

½ medium red bell pepper, sliced

½ medium green bell pepper, sliced

½ medium yellow bell pepper, sliced

1 medium onion, sliced

14 grape tomatoes

⅓ cup hoisin sauce

¼ cup water

3 tablespoons all-purpose flour

3 tablespoons soy sauce

2 teaspoons garlic powder

1 teaspoon ground cumin

1 teaspoon dried oregano

1 teaspoon paprika

⅛ teaspoon ground red pepper

Hot cooked rice (optional)

1. Heat oil in large skillet over medium-high heat. Add beef in batches; cook 4 to 5 minutes or until browned. Remove to large paper towel-lined plate.

2. Add bell peppers, onion and tomatoes to **CROCK-POT**® slow cooker. Combine hoisin sauce, water, flour, soy sauce, garlic powder, cumin, oregano, paprika and ground red pepper in medium bowl; stir to blend. Add to **CROCK-POT**® slow cooker. Top with beef. Cover; cook on LOW 8 to 9 hours or on HIGH 4 to 4½ hours. Serve with rice, if desired.

MOM'S BRISKET

MAKES 4 SERVINGS

4 teaspoons paprika, divided

1 beef brisket (about 2 pounds), scored on both sides

Olive oil

2 cups water

1½ cups ketchup

2 large onions, diced

2 tablespoons horseradish

4 Yukon Gold potatoes, peeled and cut into 1-inch pieces

2 teaspoons paprika

Salt and black pepper

1. Rub 2 teaspoons paprika evenly over beef. Heat oil in large skillet over medium heat. Brown brisket on both sides. Remove to **CROCK-POT**® slow cooker.

2. Combine water, ketchup, onions and horseradish in small bowl; stir to blend. Add to **CROCK-POT**® slow cooker. Cover; cook on LOW 7 to 9 hours or on HIGH 3 to 5 hours.

3. Remove meat to large cutting board. Cool and cut in thin diagonal slices. (At this point, meat can be refrigerated overnight.)

4. Sprinkle potatoes with remaining 2 teaspoons paprika. Place in **CROCK-POT**® slow cooker. Place sliced meat on top of potatoes. Season with salt and pepper. Cover; cook on LOW 6 to 8 hours or on HIGH 3 to 4 hours.

BRAISED LAMB SHANKS

MAKES 4 SERVINGS

4 (12- to 16-ounce) lamb shanks

¾ teaspoon salt, divided

¼ teaspoon black pepper

1 tablespoon olive oil

1 medium onion, chopped

2 stalks celery, chopped

2 carrots, chopped

6 cloves garlic, minced

1 teaspoon dried basil

1 can (about 14 ounces) diced tomatoes

2 tablespoons tomato paste

Chopped fresh Italian parsley (optional)

1. Coat inside of **CROCK-POT**® slow cooker with nonstick cooking spray. Season lamb with ½ teaspoon salt and pepper. Heat oil in large skillet over medium-high heat. Add lamb; cook 8 to 10 minutes or until browned on all sides. Remove lamb to **CROCK-POT**® slow cooker.

2. Return skillet to medium-high heat. Add onion, celery, carrots, garlic and basil; cook and stir 3 to 4 minutes or until vegetables are softened. Add tomatoes, tomato paste and remaining ¼ teaspoon salt; cook and stir 2 to 3 minutes or until slightly thickened. Pour tomato mixture over lamb shanks in **CROCK-POT**® slow cooker.

3. Cover; cook on LOW 8 to 9 hours or until lamb is very tender. Remove lamb to large serving platter; cover to keep warm. Turn **CROCK-POT**® slow cooker to HIGH. Cook, uncovered, on HIGH 10 to 15 minutes or until sauce is thickened. Serve lamb with sauce. Garnish with parsley.

CORNED BEEF AND CABBAGE

MAKES 6 SERVINGS

2 onions, thickly sliced

1 corned beef brisket (about 3 pounds) with seasoning packet

1 package (8 to 10 ounces) baby carrots

6 medium potatoes, cut into wedges

1 cup water

3 to 5 slices bacon

1 head green cabbage, cut into wedges

1. Place onions in bottom of **CROCK-POT**® slow cooker. Add corned beef with seasoning packet, carrots and potato wedges. Pour 1 cup water over top. Cover; cook on LOW 10 hours.

2. With 30 minutes left in cooking time, heat large saucepan over medium heat. Add bacon; cook and stir until crisp. Remove to paper towel-lined plate using slotted spoon. Reserve drippings in pan. Crumble bacon when cool enough to handle.

3. Place cabbage in saucepan with bacon drippings, cover with water. Bring to a boil; cook 20 to 30 minutes or until cabbage is tender. Drain. Serve corned beef with vegetables; topped with bacon.

EASY SALISBURY STEAK

MAKES 4 SERVINGS

1½ pounds ground beef

1 egg

½ cup plain dry bread crumbs

1 package (about 1 ounce) dry onion soup mix*

1 can (10½ ounces) golden mushroom soup, undiluted

*You may pulse onion soup mix in a small food processor or coffee grinder for a finer grind, if desired.

1. Coat inside of **CROCK-POT**® slow cooker with nonstick cooking spray. Combine beef, egg, bread crumbs and dry soup mix in large bowl. Form mixture evenly into four 1-inch thick patties.

2. Heat large skillet over medium-high heat. Add patties; cook 2 minutes per side until lightly browned. Remove to **CROCK-POT**® slow cooker, in single layer. Pour mushroom soup evenly over patties. Cover; cook on LOW 3 to 3½ hours.

HEARTY SANDWICHES

CAMPFIRED-UP SLOPPY JOES

MAKES 6 SERVINGS

1½ pounds ground beef

½ cup chopped sweet onion

1 medium red bell pepper, chopped

1 large clove garlic, crushed

½ cup ketchup

½ cup barbecue sauce

2 tablespoons cider vinegar

1 tablespoon Worcestershire sauce

1 tablespoon packed brown sugar

1 teaspoon chili powder

1 can (about 8 ounces) baked beans

6 Kaiser rolls, split and warmed

Shredded sharp Cheddar cheese (optional)

1. Brown beef, onion, bell pepper and garlic in large skillet over medium-high heat 6 to 8 minutes, stirring to break up meat. Remove beef mixture to **CROCK-POT**® slow cooker using slotted spoon.

2. Combine ketchup, barbecue sauce, vinegar, Worcestershire sauce, brown sugar and chili powder in small bowl. Remove to **CROCK-POT**® slow cooker.

3. Add beans; stir to combine. Cover; cook on HIGH 3 hours.

4. To serve, fill rolls evenly with sloppy joe mixture. Sprinkle with Cheddar cheese, if desired, before topping sandwich with roll top.

SERVING SUGGESTION: *Serve with a side of coleslaw.*

EASY BEEF SANDWICHES

MAKES 6 TO 8 SERVINGS

1 large onion, sliced

1 boneless beef bottom round roast (about 3 to 5 pounds)*

1 cup water

1 package (about 1 ounce) au jus gravy mix

French rolls, sliced lengthwise

Provolone cheese

*Unless you have a 5-, 6- or 7-quart **CROCK-POT®** slow cooker, cut any roast larger than 2½ pounds in half so it cooks completely.

1. Place onion slices in bottom of **CROCK-POT®** slow cooker; top with roast. Combine water and dry gravy mix in small bowl; pour over roast. Cover; cook on LOW 7 to 9 hours.

2. Remove roast to large cutting board; shred with two forks. Turn off heat. Let cooking liquid stand 5 to 10 minutes. Skim off and discard fat. Serve meat on rolls; top with cheese. Serve cooking liquid on the side for dipping.

BIG AL'S HOT AND SWEET SAUSAGE SANDWICHES

MAKES 8 TO 10 SERVINGS

4 to 5 pounds hot Italian sausage links

1 jar (24 to 26 ounces) pasta sauce

1 large Vidalia onion (or other sweet onion), sliced

1 green bell pepper, sliced

1 red bell pepper, sliced

¼ cup packed dark brown sugar

Provolone cheese, sliced

Italian rolls, split

1. Combine sausages, pasta sauce, onion, bell peppers and brown sugar in **CROCK-POT®** slow cooker. Cover; cook on LOW 8 to 10 hours or on HIGH 4 to 6 hours.

2. Place cheese in rolls; top with sausages. Top with vegetable mixture.

HOT AND JUICY REUBEN SANDWICHES

MAKES 4 SERVINGS

1 corned beef brisket, trimmed (about 1½ pounds), trimmed

2 cups sauerkraut, drained

½ cup beef broth

1 small onion, sliced

1 clove garlic, minced

¼ teaspoon caraway seeds

4 to 6 black peppercorns

8 slices pumpernickel or rye bread

4 slices Swiss cheese

Prepared mustard

1. Place corned beef, sauerkraut, broth, onion, garlic, caraway seeds and peppercorns in **CROCK-POT®** slow cooker. Cover; cook on LOW 7 to 9 hours.

2. Remove beef to large cutting board. Cut beef across grain into slices. Divide among 4 bread slices. Top each slice with drained sauerkraut mixture and 1 slice cheese. Spread mustard on remaining 4 bread slices; place on sandwiches.

BURGUNDY BEEF PO' BOYS WITH DIPPING SAUCE

MAKES 6 TO 8 SERVINGS

1 boneless beef chuck shoulder or bottom round roast (about 3 pounds), trimmed*

2 cups chopped onions

¼ cup dry red wine

3 tablespoons balsamic vinegar

1 tablespoon beef bouillon granules

1 tablespoon Worcestershire sauce

¾ teaspoon dried thyme

½ teaspoon garlic powder

Italian rolls, warmed and split

*Unless you have a 5-, 6- or 7-quart **CROCK-POT®** slow cooker, cut any roast larger than 2½ pounds in half so it cooks completely.

1. Place onions in bottom of **CROCK-POT®** slow cooker. Top with beef, wine, vinegar, bouillon granules, Worcestershire sauce, thyme and garlic powder. Cover; cook on HIGH 8 to 10 hours or until beef is very tender.

2. Remove beef to large cutting board; shred with two forks. Turn off heat. Let cooking liquid stand 5 minutes. Skim off and discard fat.

3. Spoon beef onto rolls. Serve with cooking liquid as dipping sauce.

CUBAN PORK SANDWICHES

MAKES 8 SERVINGS

1 pork loin roast
(about 2 pounds)

½ cup orange juice

2 tablespoons lime
juice

1 tablespoon minced
garlic

1½ teaspoons salt

½ teaspoon red
pepper flakes

2 tablespoons yellow
mustard

8 crusty bread rolls,
split in half
(6 inches *each*)

8 slices Swiss cheese

8 thin ham slices

4 small dill pickles,
thinly sliced
lengthwise

Nonstick cooking
spray

1. Coat inside of **CROCK-POT**® slow cooker with nonstick cooking spray. Add pork loin.

2. Combine orange juice, lime juice, garlic, salt and red pepper flakes in small bowl; stir to blend. Pour over pork. Cover; cook on LOW 7 to 8 hours or on HIGH 3½ to 4 hours. Remove pork to large cutting board. Cover loosely with foil; let stand 10 to 15 minutes before slicing.

3. To serve, spread mustard on both sides of rolls. Divide pork slices among roll bottoms. Top with Swiss cheese slice, ham slice and pickle slices; cover with top of roll.

4. Spray large skillet with nonstick cooking spray; heat over medium heat. Working in batches, arrange sandwiches in skillet. Cover with foil and top with dinner plate to press down sandwiches. (If necessary, weigh down with 2 to 3 cans to compress sandwiches lightly.) Heat 8 minutes or until cheese is slightly melted.*

Or use table top grill to compress and heat sandwiches.

GREEN CHILE PULLED PORK SANDWICHES

MAKES 8 SERVINGS

1 boneless pork shoulder roast (3½ to 4 pounds)*

1 teaspoon salt

½ teaspoon black pepper

1 can (about 14 ounces) diced tomatoes with mild green chiles

1 cup chopped onion

½ cup water

2 tablespoons lime juice

1 teaspoon ground cumin

1 teaspoon minced garlic

2 canned chipotle peppers in adobo sauce, minced

8 hard rolls or hoagie buns, split

½ cup sour cream

2 avocados, sliced

*Unless you have a 5-, 6- or 7-quart **CROCK-POT®** slow cooker, cut any roast larger than 2½ pounds in half so it cooks completely.

1. Season pork with salt and black pepper. Place pork in **CROCK-POT®** slow cooker.

2. Combine tomatoes, onion, water, lime juice, cumin, garlic and chipotle peppers in medium bowl. Pour over pork in **CROCK-POT®** slow cooker. Cover; cook on LOW 7 to 8 hours.

3. Turn off heat. Remove pork to large cutting board; cool slightly. Remove any fat from surface of meat and discard. Shred pork with two forks. Skim off and discard fat from cooking liquid. Return pork to cooking liquid; stir to combine. Serve on rolls. Top with sour cream and avocado.

PORK TENDERLOIN SLIDERS

MAKES 12 SANDWICHES

2 teaspoons chili powder

¾ teaspoon ground cumin

½ teaspoon salt

½ teaspoon black pepper

2 tablespoons olive oil, divided

2 pork tenderloins (about 1 pound *each*)

2 cups chicken broth

12 green onions, ends trimmed

½ cup mayonnaise

1 canned chipotle pepper in adobo sauce, minced

2 teaspoons lime juice

12 dinner rolls, sliced in half horizontally

12 slices Monterey Jack cheese

1. Coat inside of **CROCK-POT**® slow cooker with nonstick cooking spray. Combine chili powder, cumin, salt and black pepper in small bowl. Rub 1 tablespoon oil evenly over each pork tenderloin. Sprinkle cumin mixture evenly over tenderloins, turning to coat. Heat large skillet over medium heat. Cook tenderloins 7 to 10 minutes or until browned on all sides. Remove to **CROCK-POT**® slow cooker; add broth and green onions. Cover; cook on LOW 6 to 8 hours.

2. Combine mayonnaise, chipotle pepper and lime juice is small bowl; stir to blend. Cover and refrigerate.

3. Remove pork and green onions from **CROCK-POT**® slow cooker. Coarsely chop green onions. Thinly slice pork. Evenly spread chipotle mayonnaise on bottom halves of rolls. Top with green onions, tenderloin slices and cheese. Replace roll tops. Serve immediately.

CHICKEN AND BRIE SANDWICHES

MAKES 6 SERVINGS

1 red bell pepper, chopped

1 to 2 carrots, sliced

½ cup sliced celery

1 onion, chopped

1 clove garlic, minced

¼ teaspoon dried oregano

¼ teaspoon red pepper flakes

¼ cup all-purpose flour

1 teaspoon salt

½ teaspoon black pepper

6 boneless, skinless chicken thighs or breasts

1 tablespoon vegetable oil

1 can (about 14 ounces) chicken broth

6 sub rolls, sliced in half and toasted *or* 2 thin baguettes (about 12 ounces *each*), sliced in half and toasted

1 large wedge brie cheese, cut into 12 pieces

1. Place bell pepper, carrots, celery, onion, garlic, oregano and red pepper flakes in **CROCK-POT**® slow cooker.

2. Combine flour, salt and black pepper in large resealable food storage bag. Add chicken, 2 pieces at a time; shake to coat with flour mixture. Heat oil in large skillet over medium-high heat. Brown chicken on both sides.

3. Place chicken over vegetables in **CROCK-POT**® slow cooker; add broth. Cover; cook on LOW 5 to 6 hours.

4. Remove 1 piece of chicken from **CROCK-POT**® slow cooker, slice thinly and arrange on 1 sub roll. Spoon 1 to 2 tablespoons broth mixture over chicken and top with 2 slices cheese. Repeat with remaining chicken, bread and cheese.

SHREDDED PORK ROAST

MAKES 8 TO 10 SERVINGS

1 boneless pork shoulder (3½ to 4 pounds), well trimmed

1 medium onion, finely chopped

⅔ cup ketchup

⅓ cup water

2 tablespoons chili powder

2 tablespoons packed brown sugar

1 tablespoon ground cumin

2 teaspoons garlic powder

1 teaspoon salt

1 teaspoon Worcestershire sauce

½ teaspoon black pepper

Hoagie rolls

Carrots and celery sticks (optional)

1. Coat inside of **CROCK-POT®** slow cooker with nonstick cooking spray. Place pork shoulder in **CROCK-POT®** slow cooker. Combine onion, ketchup, water, chili powder, brown sugar, cumin, garlic powder, salt, Worcestershire sauce and pepper in medium bowl; stir to blend. Pour ketchup mixture over pork; turn to coat. Cover; cook on LOW 8 to 10 hours or on HIGH 4½ to 5 hours. Turn off heat.

2. Remove pork to large bowl; shred with two forks, discarding fat. Skim off and discard fat from cooking liquid. Pour ¾ cup cooking liquid into bowl with pork; toss well. Serve pork in rolls. Serve with carrots and celery.

NOTE: *If you like a saucier recipe, double the sauce recipe and save half for after cooking. After cooking, drain and discard cooking liquid. Shred meat; add new sauce. Cover; cook on HIGH 30 minutes or until heated through.*

JUICY REUBEN SLIDERS

MAKES 24 SLIDERS

1 corned beef brisket (about 1½ pounds), trimmed

2 cups sauerkraut, drained

½ cup beef broth

1 small onion, sliced

1 clove garlic, minced

4 to 6 whole white peppercorns

¼ teaspoon caraway seeds

48 slices pumpernickel or cocktail rye bread

12 slices deli Swiss cheese, quartered

Dijon mustard (optional)

1. Place corned beef in **CROCK-POT®** slow cooker. Add sauerkraut, broth, onion, garlic, peppercorns and caraway seeds. Cover; cook on LOW 7 to 9 hours.

2. Remove corned beef to large cutting board. Cut across grain into 16 slices. Cut each slice into 3 pieces. Place 2 pieces corned beef on each of 24 slices of bread. Place 1 heaping tablespoon sauerkraut on each sandwich. Place 2 quarters of cheese on each sandwich. Spread remaining 24 slices of bread with mustard, if desired, and place on top of sandwiches.

PHILLY CHEESE STEAKS

MAKES 8 SERVINGS

2 pounds beef round steak, sliced

4 onions, sliced

2 green bell peppers, sliced

2 tablespoons butter, melted

1 tablespoon garlic-pepper seasoning

Salt

½ cup water

2 teaspoons beef bouillon granules

8 crusty Italian or French rolls, sliced in half*

8 slices Cheddar cheese, cut in half

*Toast rolls under broiler or on griddle, if desired.

1. Combine steak, onions, bell peppers, butter, garlic-pepper seasoning and salt in **CROCK-POT**® slow cooker.

2. Whisk together water and bouillon in small bowl; pour into **CROCK-POT**® slow cooker. Cover; cook on LOW 6 to 8 hours.

3. Remove beef, onions and bell peppers from **CROCK-POT**® slow cooker. Place beef mixture in rolls. Top with cheese; place under broiler until cheese is melted, if desired.

BEST BEEF BRISKET SANDWICH EVER

MAKES 12 SERVINGS

1 well-trimmed, lean beef brisket (about 3 pounds)*

2 cups apple cider, divided

1 head garlic, cloves separated and crushed

2 tablespoons whole peppercorns

⅓ cup chopped fresh thyme *or* 2 tablespoons dried thyme

1 tablespoon mustard seeds

1 tablespoon Cajun seasoning

1 teaspoon ground allspice

1 teaspoon ground cumin

1 teaspoon celery seeds

2 to 4 whole cloves

1 can (12 ounces) dark beer

12 sourdough sandwich rolls, sliced in half

*Unless you have a 5-, 6- or 7-quart **CROCK-POT®** slow cooker, cut any roast larger than 2½ pounds in half so it cooks completely.

1. Place brisket, ½ cup cider, garlic, peppercorns, thyme, mustard seeds, Cajun seasoning, allspice, cumin, celery seeds and cloves in large resealable food storage bag. Seal bag; marinate in refrigerator overnight.

2. Place brisket and marinade in **CROCK-POT®** slow cooker. Add remaining 1½ cups apple cider and beer. Cover; cook on LOW 10 hours.

3. Strain sauce; drizzle over meat. Slice brisket and place on sandwich rolls.

MINI SWISS STEAK SANDWICHES

MAKES 16 TO 18 SERVINGS

2 tablespoons all-purpose flour

¼ teaspoon salt

¼ teaspoon black pepper

1¾ pounds boneless beef chuck steak, about 1 inch thick

2 tablespoons vegetable oil

1 medium onion, sliced

1 green bell pepper, sliced

1 clove garlic, sliced

1 cup stewed tomatoes

¾ cup condensed beef broth, undiluted

2 teaspoons Worcestershire sauce

1 whole bay leaf

2 tablespoons cornstarch

2 packages (12 ounces *each*) sweet Hawaiian-style dinner rolls

1. Coat inside of **CROCK-POT®** slow cooker with nonstick cooking spray. Combine flour, salt and black pepper in large resealable food storage bag. Add steak. Seal bag; shake to coat.

2. Heat oil in large skillet over high heat. Brown steak on both sides. Remove to **CROCK-POT®** slow cooker.

3. Add onion and bell pepper to skillet; cook and stir over medium-high heat 3 minutes or until softened. Add garlic; cook and stir 30 seconds. Pour mixture over steak.

4. Add tomatoes, broth, Worcestershire sauce and bay leaf to **CROCK-POT®** slow cooker. Cover; cook on HIGH 3½ hours or until steak is tender. Remove steak to large cutting board. Remove and discard bay leaf.

5. Stir 2 tablespoons cooking liquid into cornstarch in small bowl until smooth. Whisk into cooking liquid in **CROCK-POT®** slow cooker. Cover; cook on HIGH 10 minutes or until thickened.

6. Thinly slice steak against the grain to shred. Return steak to **CROCK-POT®** slow cooker; mix well. Serve steak mixture on rolls.

TIP: *Browning meat and poultry before cooking them in the* **CROCK-POT®** *slow cooker is not necessary, but helps to enhance the flavor and appearance of the finished dish.*

MEATBALL GRINDERS

MAKES 4 SERVINGS

1 can (about 14 ounces) diced tomatoes

1 can (8 ounces) tomato sauce

¼ cup chopped onion

2 tablespoons tomato paste

1 teaspoon Italian seasoning

1 pound ground chicken

½ cup fresh whole wheat or white bread crumbs (1 slice bread)

1 egg white, lightly beaten

3 tablespoons finely chopped fresh parsley

2 cloves garlic, minced

¼ teaspoon salt

⅛ teaspoon black pepper

Nonstick cooking spray

4 small hard rolls, split

2 tablespoons grated Parmesan cheese

1. Combine tomatoes, tomato sauce, onion, tomato paste and Italian seasoning in **CROCK-POT®** slow cooker. Cover; cook on LOW 3 to 4 hours.

2. Halfway through cooking time, prepare meatballs. Combine chicken, bread crumbs, egg white, parsley, garlic, salt and pepper in medium bowl. Form mixture into 12 to 16 meatballs. Spray medium skillet with cooking spray; heat over medium heat. Add meatballs; cook 8 to 10 minutes or until well browned on all sides. Remove meatballs to **CROCK-POT®** slow cooker.

3. Cover; cook on LOW 1 to 2 hours or until meatballs are no longer pink in centers and are heated through. Place 3 to 4 meatballs in each roll. Spoon sauce over meatballs. Sprinkle with cheese.

BARBECUE FAVORITES

BARBECUE TURKEY LEGS

MAKES 6 SERVINGS

6 turkey drumsticks

2 teaspoons salt

2 teaspoons black pepper

½ cup white vinegar

½ cup ketchup

½ cup molasses

¼ cup Worcestershire sauce

1 tablespoon onion powder

1 tablespoon garlic powder

1 teaspoon hickory liquid smoke

⅛ teaspoon chipotle chili powder

1. Season drumsticks with salt and pepper. Place in **CROCK-POT**® slow cooker.

2. Combine vinegar, ketchup, molasses, Worcestershire sauce, onion powder, garlic powder, liquid smoke and chili powder in medium bowl; stir to blend. Add to **CROCK-POT**® slow cooker; turn drumsticks to coat. Cover; cook on LOW 7 to 8 hours or on HIGH 3 to 4 hours.

BARBECUED BEEF SANDWICHES

MAKES 12 SERVINGS

2 cups ketchup

1 onion, chopped

¼ cup cider vinegar

¼ cup dark molasses

2 tablespoons Worcestershire sauce

2 cloves garlic, minced

½ teaspoon ground mustard

½ teaspoon black pepper

¼ teaspoon garlic powder

¼ teaspoon red pepper flakes

1 boneless beef chuck shoulder roast (about 3 pounds), trimmed*

12 sesame seed buns

*Unless you have a 5-, 6- or 7-quart **CROCK-POT®** slow cooker, cut any roast larger than 2½ pounds in half so it cooks completely.

1. Combine ketchup, onion, vinegar, molasses, Worcestershire sauce, garlic, mustard, black pepper, garlic powder and red pepper flakes in **CROCK-POT®** slow cooker; stir to blend. Place beef in **CROCK-POT®** slow cooker. Cover; cook on LOW 8 to 10 hours or on HIGH 4 to 5 hours.

2. Turn off heat. Remove beef to large cutting board; shred with two forks. Let cooking liquid stand 5 minutes. Skim off and discard fat.

3. Add shredded beef; stir to coat. Cover; cook on HIGH 15 to 30 minutes or until heated through. Spoon filling into buns; top with additional sauce, if desired.

TEXAS-STYLE BARBECUED BRISKET

MAKES 10 TO 12 SERVINGS

3 tablespoons Worcestershire sauce

1 tablespoon chili powder

1 teaspoon celery salt

1 teaspoon black pepper

1 teaspoon liquid smoke

2 cloves garlic, minced

1 beef brisket (3 to 4 pounds), trimmed*

2 whole bay leaves

1¾ cups barbecue sauce, plus additional for serving

*Unless you have a 5-, 6- or 7-quart **CROCK-POT**® slow cooker, cut any roast larger than 2½ pounds in half so it cooks completely.

1. Combine Worcestershire sauce, chili powder, celery salt, pepper, liquid smoke and garlic in small bowl; stir to blend. Spread mixture on all sides of beef. Place beef in large resealable food storage bag; seal bag. Refrigerate 24 hours.

2. Place beef, marinade and bay leaves in **CROCK-POT**® slow cooker. Cover; cook on LOW 7 hours.

3. Remove beef to large cutting board. Turn off heat. Pour cooking liquid into 2-cup measure; let stand 5 minutes. Skim off and discard fat. Remove and discard bay leaves. Stir 1 cup juice into 1¾ cups barbecue sauce in medium bowl. Discard any remaining juice in **CROCK-POT**® slow cooker.

4. Return beef and barbecue sauce mixture to **CROCK-POT**® slow cooker. Cover; cook on LOW 1 hour or until meat is fork-tender. Remove beef to large cutting board. Cut across grain into ¼-inch-thick slices. Serve with additional barbecue sauce.

ROOT BEER BBQ PULLED PORK

MAKES 8 SERVINGS

1 can (12 ounces) root beer

1 bottle (18 ounces) sweet barbecue sauce, divided

1 package (1 ounce) dry onion soup mix

1 boneless pork shoulder roast (6 to 8 pounds)

Salt and black pepper

Hamburger buns

*Unless you have a 5-, 6- or 7-quart **CROCK-POT®** slow cooker, cut any roast larger than 2½ pounds in half so it cooks completely.

1. Coat inside of **CROCK-POT®** slow cooker with nonstick cooking spray. Combine root beer and ½ bottle barbecue sauce in medium bowl. Rub dry soup mix on pork roast. Place barbecue mixture and roast in **CROCK-POT®** slow cooker. Cover; cook on LOW 8 to 10 hours.

2. Remove pork to large cutting board; shred with two forks. Reserve 1 cup barbecue mixture in **CROCK-POT®** slow cooker; discard remaining mixture. Turn **CROCK-POT®** slow cooker to HIGH. Stir shredded pork, remaining ½ bottle barbecue sauce, salt and pepper into **CROCK-POT®** slow cooker. Cover; cook on HIGH 20 minutes or until heated through. Serve on buns.

ASIAN BARBECUE SKEWERS

MAKES 4 TO 6 SERVINGS

2 pounds boneless, skinless chicken thighs

½ cup soy sauce

⅓ cup packed brown sugar

2 tablespoons sesame oil

3 cloves garlic, minced

½ cup thinly sliced green onions (optional)

1 tablespoon toasted sesame seeds (optional)*

*To toast sesame seeds, spread in small skillet. Shake skillet over medium-low heat 2 minutes or until seeds begin to pop and turn golden brown.

1. Cut each chicken thigh into four pieces, about 1½ inches thick. Thread chicken onto 7-inch-long wooden skewers, folding thinner pieces, if necessary. Place skewers into **CROCK-POT**® slow cooker, layering as flat as possible.

2. Combine soy sauce, brown sugar, oil and garlic in small bowl; stir to blend. Reserve ⅓ cup sauce; set aside. Pour remaining sauce over skewers. Cover; cook on LOW 2 hours. Turn skewers over. Cover; cook on LOW 1 hour.

3. Remove skewers to large serving platter. Discard cooking liquid. Pour reserved sauce over skewers. Sprinkle with green onions and sesame seeds, if desired.

BARBECUE BEEF SLIDERS

MAKES 6 SERVINGS

1 tablespoon packed light brown sugar

1 teaspoon ground cumin

1 teaspoon chili powder

1 teaspoon paprika

½ teaspoon salt

¼ teaspoon ground red pepper

3 pounds beef short ribs

½ cup plus 2 tablespoons barbecue sauce, divided

¼ cup water

12 slider rolls

¾ cup prepared coleslaw

6 bread and butter pickle chips

1. Coat inside of **CROCK-POT**® slow cooker with nonstick cooking spray. Combine brown sugar, cumin, chili powder, paprika, salt and ground red pepper in small bowl; stir to blend. Rub over ribs; remove to **CROCK-POT**® slow cooker. Pour in ½ cup barbecue sauce and ¼ cup water.

2. Cover; cook on LOW 7 to 8 hours or on HIGH 4 to 4½ hours or until ribs are very tender and meat shreds easily. Remove ribs to large cutting board and discard bones; transfer to large bowl. Shred meat using two forks, discarding any large pieces of fat. Stir in remaining 2 tablespoons barbecue sauce and 2 tablespoons liquid from **CROCK-POT**® slow cooker.

3. Arrange bottom half of rolls on platter or work surface. Top each with ¼ cup beef mixture, 1 tablespoon coleslaw and 1 pickle chip. Place roll tops on each.

TIP: *To make cleanup easier, coat the inside of the* **CROCK-POT**® *slow cooker with nonstick cooking spray before adding the ingredients. To remove any sticky barbecue sauce residue, soak the stoneware in hot sudsy water, then scrub it with a plastic or nylon scrubber. Don't use steel wool.*

SIMPLE BARBECUE CHICKEN

MAKES 8 SERVINGS

- 1 bottle (20 ounces) ketchup
- ⅔ cup packed brown sugar
- ⅔ cup cider vinegar
- 2 tablespoons chili powder
- 2 tablespoons tomato paste
- 1 tablespoon onion powder
- 2 teaspoons garlic powder
- 2 teaspoons liquid smoke (optional)
- 1 teaspoon hot pepper sauce (optional)
- 8 boneless, skinless chicken breasts (6 ounces *each*)
- 8 whole wheat rolls (optional)

1. Combine ketchup, brown sugar, vinegar, chili powder, tomato paste, onion powder, garlic powder, liquid smoke, if desired, and hot pepper sauce, if desired, in **CROCK-POT**® slow cooker; stir to blend.

2. Add chicken. Cover; cook on LOW 4 to 6 hours or on HIGH 2 to 3 hours or until chicken is cooked through. Serve with rolls, if desired.

CHILI BARBECUE BEANS

MAKES 8 TO 10 SERVINGS

1 cup dried Great Northern beans, rinsed and sorted

1 cup dried red beans or dried kidney beans, rinsed and sorted

1 cup dried baby lima beans, rinsed and sorted

3 cups water

8 slices bacon, crisp-cooked and crumbled *or* 8 ounces smoked sausage, sliced

¼ cup packed brown sugar

2 tablespoons minced onion

2 cubes beef bouillon

1 teaspoon dry mustard

1 teaspoon chili powder

1 teaspoon minced garlic

½ teaspoon black pepper

¼ teaspoon red pepper flakes

2 whole bay leaves

1 to 1½ cups barbecue sauce

1. Place beans in large bowl and add enough cold water to cover by at least 2 inches. Soak 6 to 8 hours or overnight.* Drain beans; discard water.

2. Combine soaked beans, 3 cups water, bacon, brown sugar, onion, bouillon cubes, dry mustard, chili powder, garlic, black pepper, red pepper flakes and bay leaves in **CROCK-POT®** slow cooker. Cover; cook on LOW 8 to 10 hours.

3. Stir in barbecue sauce. Cover; cook on LOW 1 hour or until heated through. Remove and discard bay leaves.

To quick soak beans, place beans in large saucepan. Cover with water. Bring to a boil over high heat. Boil 2 minutes. Remove from heat; let soak, covered, 1 hour.

HOISIN BARBECUE CHICKEN THIGHS

MAKES 6 TO 8 SERVINGS

⅔ cup hoisin sauce

⅓ cup barbecue sauce

3 tablespoons quick-cooking tapioca

1 tablespoon sugar

1 tablespoon soy sauce

¼ teaspoon red pepper flakes

12 skinless, bone-in chicken thighs (3½ to 4 pounds)

1½ pounds uncooked ramen noodles or other pasta

Sliced green onions (optional)

1. Stir hoisin sauce, barbecue sauce, tapioca, sugar, soy sauce and red pepper flakes in **CROCK-POT**® slow cooker until blended. Add chicken flesh side down. Cover; cook on LOW 8 to 9 hours.

2. Meanwhile, cook ramen noodles according to package directions. Serve chicken over noodles. Garnish with green onions.

PULLED PORK SLIDERS WITH COLA BARBECUE SAUCE

MAKES 16 SLIDERS

1 teaspoon vegetable oil

1 boneless pork shoulder roast (3 pounds), cut evenly into 4 pieces*

1 cup cola

¼ cup tomato paste

2 tablespoons packed brown sugar

2 teaspoons Worcestershire sauce

2 teaspoons spicy brown mustard

Hot pepper sauce

Salt

16 dinner rolls or potato rolls

Sliced pickles (optional)

*Unless you have a 5-, 6- or 7-quart **CROCK-POT®** slow cooker, cut any roast larger than 2½ pounds in half so it cooks completely.

1. Heat oil in large skillet over medium-high heat. Brown pork on all sides. Remove to **CROCK-POT®** slow cooker. Pour cola over pork. Cover; cook on LOW 7½ to 8 hours or on HIGH 3½ to 4 hours.

2. Turn off heat. Remove pork to large cutting board; shred with two forks. Let cooking liquid stand 5 minutes. Skim off and discard fat. Whisk tomato paste, brown sugar, Worcestershire sauce and mustard into cooking liquid. Cover; cook on HIGH 15 minutes or until thickened.

3. Stir shredded pork into **CROCK-POT®** slow cooker. Season with hot pepper sauce and salt. Serve on rolls. Top with pickles, if desired.

BARBECUE FAVORITES

TURKEY MEATBALLS IN CRANBERRY-BARBECUE SAUCE

MAKES 12 SERVINGS

1 can (16 ounces) jellied cranberry sauce

½ cup barbecue sauce

1 egg

1 pound ground turkey

1 green onion, sliced

2 teaspoons grated orange peel

1 teaspoon soy sauce

¼ teaspoon black pepper

⅛ teaspoon ground red pepper (optional)

Nonstick cooking spray

1. Combine cranberry sauce and barbecue sauce in **CROCK-POT®** slow cooker. Cover; cook on HIGH 20 to 30 minutes or until cranberry sauce melts and mixture is heated through.

2. Meanwhile, place egg in large bowl; beat lightly. Add turkey, green onion, orange peel, soy sauce, black pepper and ground red pepper, if desired; mix until well blended. Shape into 24 meatballs.

3. Spray large skillet with cooking spray. Add meatballs; cook over medium heat 8 to 10 minutes or until meatballs are browned. Add to **CROCK-POT®** slow cooker; stir gently to coat.

4. Turn **CROCK-POT®** slow cooker to LOW. Cover; cook on LOW 3 hours.

BBQ PULLED CHICKEN SANDWICHES

MAKES 6 SERVINGS

1¼ to 1½ pounds boneless, skinless chicken thighs

¾ cup barbecue sauce, divided

1 package (14 ounces) frozen bell pepper and onion strips cut for stir-fry

¼ to ½ teaspoon hot pepper sauce

6 Kaiser rolls, split in half and toasted

Dill pickle spears (optional)

1. Combine chicken and ¼ cup barbecue sauce in **CROCK-POT®** slow cooker; mix well. Add bell pepper and onion strips; mix well. Cover; cook on LOW 5 to 6 hours or on HIGH 2 to 3 hours.

2. Remove chicken to medium bowl; shred with two forks. Drain pepper mixture; add to bowl with chicken. Add remaining ½ cup barbecue sauce and hot pepper sauce; mix well. Serve in rolls with pickles, if desired.

KOREAN BARBECUE BEEF

MAKES 6 SERVINGS

4 to 4½ pounds beef short ribs

¼ cup chopped green onions

¼ cup tamari or soy sauce

¼ cup beef broth

1 tablespoon packed brown sugar

2 teaspoons minced fresh ginger

2 teaspoons minced garlic

½ teaspoon black pepper

2 teaspoons dark sesame oil

Hot cooked rice

2 teaspoons sesame seeds, toasted*

*To toast sesame seeds, spread in small skillet. Shake skillet over medium-low heat 2 minutes or until seeds begin to pop and turn golden brown.

1. Place ribs in **CROCK-POT®** slow cooker. Combine green onions, tamari, broth, brown sugar, ginger, garlic and pepper in medium bowl; stir to blend. Pour over ribs. Cover; cook on LOW 7 to 8 hours or until ribs are fork-tender.

2. Turn off heat. Remove ribs from cooking liquid. Cool slightly. Trim excess fat and discard. Cut rib meat into bite-size pieces, discarding bones.

3. Let cooking liquid stand 5 minutes to allow fat to rise. Skim off and discard fat. Stir sesame oil into cooking liquid.

4. Return beef to cooking liquid in **CROCK-POT®** slow cooker. Cover; cook on LOW 15 to 30 minutes or until heated through. Serve over rice; sprinkle with sesame seeds.

PULLED PORK WITH HONEY-CHIPOTLE BARBECUE SAUCE

MAKES 8 SERVINGS

1 tablespoon chili powder, divided

1 teaspoon chipotle chili powder, divided

1 teaspoon ground cumin, divided

1 teaspoon garlic powder, divided

1 teaspoon salt

1 bone-in pork shoulder (3½ pounds), trimmed

1 can (15 ounces) tomato sauce

5 tablespoons honey, divided

1. Coat inside of **CROCK-POT®** slow cooker with nonstick cooking spray. Combine 1 teaspoon chili powder, ½ teaspoon chipotle chili powder, ½ teaspoon cumin, ½ teaspoon garlic powder and salt in small bowl. Rub pork with chili powder mixture. Place pork in **CROCK-POT®** slow cooker.

2. Combine tomato sauce, 4 tablespoons honey, remaining 2 teaspoons chili powder, ½ teaspoon chipotle chili powder, ½ teaspoon cumin and ½ teaspoon garlic powder in large bowl; stir to blend. Pour tomato mixture over pork in **CROCK-POT®** slow cooker. Cover; cook on LOW 8 hours. Turn off heat.

3. Remove pork to large bowl; cover loosely with foil. Let sauce in **CROCK-POT®** slow cooker stand 5 minutes. Skim off and discard fat. Turn **CROCK-POT®** slow cooker to HIGH. Cover; cook on HIGH 30 minutes or until sauce is thickened. Stir in remaining 1 tablespoon honey. Turn off heat.

4. Remove bone from pork and discard. Shred pork using two forks. Stir shredded pork back into **CROCK-POT®** slow cooker to coat well with sauce.

HOISIN BARBECUE CHICKEN SLIDERS

MAKES 16 SLIDERS

⅔ cup hoisin sauce

⅓ cup barbecue sauce

3 tablespoons quick-cooking tapioca

1 tablespoon sugar

1 tablespoon soy sauce

¼ teaspoon red pepper flakes

12 boneless, skinless chicken thighs (3 to 3½ pounds total)

16 dinner rolls or Hawaiian sweet rolls, split

½ medium red onion, finely chopped (optional)

Sliced pickles (optional)

1. Combine hoisin sauce, barbecue sauce, tapioca, sugar, soy sauce and red pepper flakes in **CROCK-POT**® slow cooker; stir to blend. Add chicken. Cover; cook on LOW 8 to 9 hours.

2. Remove chicken to large cutting board; shred with two forks. Return shredded chicken to **CROCK-POT**® slow cooker; stir well. Spoon chicken and sauce evenly onto bottom roll. Top each with chopped onion and pickles, if desired, and top roll.

COOKING WITH BEER

CERVEZA CHICKEN ENCHILADA CASSEROLE

MAKES 4 TO 6 SERVINGS

2 cups water

1 stalk celery, chopped

1 small carrot, chopped

1 can (12 ounces) Mexican beer, divided

Juice of 1 lime

1 teaspoon salt

1½ pounds boneless, skinless chicken breasts

1 can (19 ounces) enchilada sauce

7 ounces white corn tortilla chips

½ medium onion, chopped

3 cups (12 ounces) shredded Cheddar cheese

Optional toppings: sour cream, sliced black olives and chopped fresh cilantro

1. Bring water, celery, carrot, 1 cup beer, lime juice and salt to a boil in large saucepan over high heat. Add chicken breasts; reduce heat to simmer. Cook 12 to 14 minutes or until chicken is cooked through. Remove chicken to large cutting board; shred into 1-inch pieces.

2. Spread ½ cup enchilada sauce in bottom of **CROCK-POT**® slow cooker. Arrange one third of tortilla chips over sauce. Layer with one third of shredded chicken and one third of chopped onion. Sprinkle with 1 cup cheese. Repeat layers two times.

3. Pour remaining beer over casserole. Cover; cook on LOW 3½ to 4 hours. Top as desired.

FALL BEEF AND BEER CASSEROLE

MAKES 4 TO 6 SERVINGS

2 tablespoons oil

1½ pounds cubed beef stew meat

2 tablespoons all-purpose flour

1 cup beef broth

2 cups brown ale or beer

1 cup water

1 onion, sliced

2 carrots, sliced

1 leek, sliced

2 stalks celery, sliced

1 cup mushrooms, sliced

1 turnip, peeled and cubed

Salt and black pepper

1. Heat oil in large skillet over medium-high heat. Cook beef until browned on all sides. Remove to **CROCK-POT**® slow cooker.

2. Sprinkle flour over contents of skillet. Cook and stir 2 minutes. Gradually stir in broth, ale and water (adding liquid ingredients too fast could create lumps in the sauce). Bring to a boil and then pour over beef.

3. Add onion, carrots, leek, celery, mushrooms, turnip, salt and pepper to **CROCK-POT**® slow cooker. Cover; cook on LOW 8 to 10 hours or on HIGH 4 to 6 hours.

SEAFOOD BOUILLABAISSE

MAKES 4 SERVINGS

Nonstick cooking spray

½ bulb fennel, chopped

1 medium onion, chopped

2 cloves garlic, minced

1 can (28 ounces) tomato purée

2 cans (12 ounces *each*) beer

2 cups water

8 ounces clam juice

1 whole bay leaf

½ teaspoon salt

¼ teaspoon black pepper

½ pound red snapper, cut into 1-inch pieces

8 mussels, scrubbed and debearded

8 cherrystone clams

8 large raw shrimp, unpeeled and rinsed (with tails on)

Lemon wedges

1. Spray large skillet with cooking spray; heat over medium-high heat. Add fennel, onion and garlic; cook and stir 5 minutes or until onion is soft and translucent. Remove fennel mixture to **CROCK-POT**® slow cooker. Add tomato purée, beer, water, clam juice, bay leaf, salt and pepper to **CROCK-POT**® slow cooker. Cover; cook on LOW 6 to 8 hours or on HIGH 3 to 4 hours.

2. Add fish, mussels, clams and shrimp to **CROCK-POT**® slow cooker. Cover; cook on LOW 15 minutes or until fish flakes when tested with fork. Discard any mussels and clams that do not open.

3. Remove and discard bay leaf. Ladle broth into wide soup bowls; top with fish, mussels, clams and shrimp. Squeeze lemon over each serving.

BEER CHICKEN

MAKES 4 TO 6 SERVINGS

2 tablespoons olive oil

1 cut-up whole chicken (3 to 5 pounds)

10 new potatoes, cut in halves

1 can (12 ounces) beer

2 medium carrots, sliced

1 cup chopped celery

1 medium onion, chopped

1 tablespoon chopped fresh rosemary

Heat oil in large skillet over medium heat. Add chicken; cook 5 to 7 minutes on each side or until browned. Remove to **CROCK-POT**® slow cooker. Add potatoes, beer, carrots, celery, onion and rosemary to **CROCK-POT**® slow cooker. Cover; cook on HIGH 5 hours.

ALE'D PORK AND SAUERKRAUT

MAKES 6 TO 8 SERVINGS

1 jar (32 ounces) sauerkraut, undrained

1½ tablespoons sugar

1 can (12 ounces) ale or dark beer

1 boneless pork shoulder or pork butt roast (3½ pounds)

½ teaspoon salt

½ teaspoon paprika

¼ teaspoon garlic powder

¼ teaspoon black pepper

*Unless you have a 5-, 6- or 7-quart **CROCK-POT**® slow cooker, cut any roast larger than 2½ pounds in half so it cooks completely.

1. Place sauerkraut in **CROCK-POT**® slow cooker. Sprinkle with sugar; add ale. Place pork, fat side up, on top of sauerkraut mixture; sprinkle evenly with salt, paprika, garlic powder and black pepper.

2. Cover; cook on HIGH 6 hours. Remove pork to large serving platter. Remove sauerkraut using slotted spoon; arrange around pork. Spoon cooking liquid over sauerkraut as desired.

SLOW COOKER SALMON WITH BEER

MAKES 4 SERVINGS

4 salmon fillets
(6 ounces *each*)

Salt and black
pepper

1 cup Italian dressing

3 tablespoons olive oil

1 yellow bell pepper,
sliced

1 red bell pepper,
sliced

1 orange bell pepper,
sliced

1 large onion, sliced

2 cloves garlic, minced

1 teaspoon lemon
peel

½ teaspoon dried basil

2 cups spinach, stems
removed

¾ cup amber ale

½ lemon, cut into
quarters

Coarse salt
(optional)

1. Season both sides of fillets with salt and black pepper. Place fillets in baking dish; pour Italian dressing over fillets. Cover; refrigerate 30 minutes or up to 2 hours. Discard marinade.

2. Pour oil into **CROCK-POT**® slow cooker; lay salmon fillets on top of oil, stacking as necessary. Top with bell peppers, onion, garlic, lemon peel and basil. Cover with spinach. Pour ale over all ingredients in **CROCK-POT**® slow cooker. Cover; cook on HIGH 1½ hours.

3. Remove fillets to large serving platter; top with vegetables. Squeeze lemon over salmon. Sprinkle with coarse salt, if desired.

BEER BOLOGNESE

MAKES 6 TO 8 SERVINGS

3 slices bacon, chopped

1 large onion, chopped

1 stalk celery, chopped

1 carrot, chopped

2 cloves garlic, minced

3 teaspoons olive oil, divided

8 ounces mushrooms, sliced

¾ pound ground beef

¾ pound ground pork

1 can (28 ounces) tomato purée

1 bottle (12 ounces) dark beer

1 cup beef broth

1 tablespoon tomato paste

1 teaspoon salt

¼ teaspoon black pepper

¼ teaspoon red pepper flakes

Hot cooked pasta

Shaved Parmesan cheese and chopped fresh parsley (optional)

1. Cook bacon in large skillet over medium-high heat. Drain on paper towels.

2. Add onion, celery and carrot to same skillet; cook and stir 5 minutes or until beginning to brown. Add garlic; cook and stir 1 to 2 minutes. Remove vegetables to **CROCK-POT**® slow cooker. Add 1 teaspoon oil to skillet. Add mushrooms; cook and stir until beginning to brown. Remove to **CROCK-POT**® slow cooker.

3. Heat remaining 2 teaspoons oil in skillet. Brown beef and pork over medium-high heat, stirring to break up meat. Drain fat. Remove meat to **CROCK-POT**® slow cooker. Add bacon, tomato purée, beer, broth, tomato paste, salt, black pepper and red pepper flakes.

4. Cover; cook on LOW 8 to 10 hours. Serve over pasta. Top with Parmesan and parsley, if desired.

CHICKEN CURRY WITH BEER

MAKES 4 TO 6 SERVINGS

⅓ cup vegetable oil

1 cut-up whole chicken (4 pounds)

1 cup chicken broth

1 cup beer

1 cup tomato sauce

1 large onion, chopped

1 tablespoon minced ginger

2½ teaspoons curry powder

1 teaspoon salt

1 teaspoon garam masala

2 cloves garlic, minced

½ teaspoon chili powder

⅛ teaspoon ground red pepper

4 cups hot cooked basmati rice

1. Heat oil in large skillet over medium-high heat. Add chicken in batches and cook until browned on all sides.

2. Remove chicken to **CROCK-POT**® slow cooker. Add broth, beer, tomato sauce, onion, ginger, curry powder, salt, garam masala, garlic, chili powder and ground red pepper; stir to blend.

3. Cover; cook on LOW 8 hours. Serve chicken with sauce over rice.

BEEF CHUCK CHILI

MAKES 8 TO 10 SERVINGS

½ cup plus 2 tablespoons olive oil, divided

1 beef chuck roast (5 pounds), trimmed*

3 cups finely chopped onions

2 green bell peppers, chopped

4 poblano peppers, seeded and finely chopped**

2 serrano peppers, seeded and minced**

3 jalapeño peppers, seeded and minced**

2 tablespoons minced garlic

1 can (28 ounces) crushed tomatoes, undrained

½ cup Mexican lager

¼ cup hot pepper sauce

1 tablespoon ground cumin

Corn bread or hot cooked rice

*Unless you have a 5-, 6- or 7-quart **CROCK-POT**® slow cooker, cut any roast larger than 2½ pounds in half so it cooks completely.

**Poblano, serrano and jalapeño peppers can sting and irritate the skin. Wear rubber gloves when handling peppers and do not touch your eyes.

1. Heat ½ cup oil in large skillet over medium-high heat. Add roast; brown on both sides. Remove to **CROCK-POT**® slow cooker.

2. Heat remaining 2 tablespoons oil in same skillet over low heat. Add onions, peppers and garlic; cook and stir 7 minutes or until onions are tender. Remove to **CROCK-POT**® slow cooker. Stir in tomatoes. Cover; cook on LOW 4 to 5 hours or until beef is fork-tender.

3. Remove beef to large cutting board; shred with two forks. Add lager, hot pepper sauce and cumin to cooking liquid. Return beef to cooking liquid; mix well. Serve over corn bread or rice.

VEAL POT ROAST

MAKES 4 TO 6 SERVINGS

2 tablespoons olive oil

1 veal shoulder roast
(2½ pounds)

Salt and black pepper

2 cloves garlic, slivered

¾ pound pearl onions,
peeled (see Tip)

½ cup sliced fennel

1 package (3.5 ounces)
shiitake mushrooms,
sliced

6 plum tomatoes,
quartered

2 cups chicken broth

1 cup light beer

1 teaspoon minced fresh
herbs (rosemary
leaves, thyme and
sage)

¼ teaspoon red pepper
flakes

¼ teaspoon grated
lemon peel

Hot cooked rice
(optional)

1. Heat oil in large skillet over medium-high heat. Season roast with salt and black pepper; add to skillet. Brown on all sides. Remove to **CROCK-POT®** slow cooker. Push garlic slivers into roast.

2. Add onions, fennel, mushrooms and tomatoes to **CROCK-POT®** slow cooker. Pour broth and beer over roast. Sprinkle herbs, red pepper flakes and lemon peel over roast.

3. Cover; cook on LOW 8 to 10 hours or until tender. Remove roast to large serving platter; let rest 10 minutes. Slice roast. Serve with vegetables, sauce and rice, if desired.

TIP: *To peel pearl onions, place in a large pot of boiling water and cook 1 minute. Drain well and run under cold water to cool slightly. Rub lightly, if necessary. The skins should come off easily.*

COOKING WITH **BEER**

BEEF CABBAGE ROLLS WITH BEER

MAKES ABOUT 12 ROLLS

12 ounces ground beef

12 ounces ground pork

1 medium onion, chopped

1 can (15 ounces) tomato sauce, divided

1 teaspoon salt

1 teaspoon dried thyme

¼ teaspoon black pepper

1 large head green cabbage

1 bottle (12 ounces) beer

Chopped fresh Italian parsley (optional)

1. Combine beef, pork, onion, 1 cup tomato sauce, salt, thyme and pepper in large bowl; stir to blend. Pour ¼ cup tomato sauce into **CROCK-POT**® slow cooker.

2. Cut out core from cabbage and carefully remove leaves. Place a golf ball-sized mound of meat mixture in center of large cabbage leaf, edges curling upward. Starting with the thickest side, fold leaf over meat mixture, burrito-style. Place, fold side down, in **CROCK-POT**® slow cooker. Repeat with remaining meat and cabbage leaves, stacking as necessary.

3. Pour beer over cabbage rolls. Pour remaining tomato sauce on top of rolls.

4. Cover; cook on LOW 5 hours. Halfway through cooking time, push cabbage rolls under liquid to submerge. Sprinkle with parsley, if desired.

TIP: *For a thicker sauce, remove cabbage rolls and add 2 tablespoons cornstarch to remaining liquid. Bring to a boil. Cook until desired thickness.*

SLOW COOKER BRISKET OF BEEF

MAKES 10 TO 12 SERVINGS

1 whole beef brisket (about 5 pounds)*

2 teaspoons minced garlic

½ teaspoon black pepper

2 large onions, cut into ¼-inch slices and separated into rings

1 bottle (12 ounces) chili sauce

12 ounces dark ale

2 tablespoons Worcestershire sauce

1 tablespoon packed brown sugar

*Unless you have a 5-, 6- or 7-quart **CROCK-POT**® slow cooker, cut any roast larger than 2½ pounds in half so it cooks completely.

1. Place brisket, fat side down, in **CROCK-POT**® slow cooker. Spread garlic evenly over brisket; sprinkle with pepper. Arrange onions over brisket. Combine chili sauce, ale, Worcestershire sauce and brown sugar in medium bowl; pour over brisket and onions. Cover; cook on LOW 8 hours.

2. Turn brisket over; stir onions into sauce and spoon over brisket. Cover; cook on LOW 1 to 2 hours or until brisket is fork-tender. Remove brisket to large cutting board. Cover loosely with foil; let stand 10 minutes.

3. Turn off heat. Stir cooking liquid; let stand 5 minutes. Skim off and discard fat. Carve brisket across the grain into thin slices. Spoon cooking liquid over brisket.

HEARTY PORK AND BACON CHILI

MAKES 8 TO 10 SERVINGS

2½ pounds pork shoulder, cut into 1-inch pieces

3½ teaspoons salt, divided

1¼ teaspoons black pepper, divided

1 tablespoon vegetable oil

4 slices thick-cut bacon, diced

2 medium onions, chopped

1 red bell pepper, chopped

¼ cup chili powder

2 tablespoons tomato paste

1 tablespoon minced garlic

1 tablespoon ground cumin

1 tablespoon smoked paprika

1 bottle (12 ounces) pale ale

2 cans (about 14 ounces *each*) diced tomatoes

2 cups water

¾ cup dried kidney beans, rinsed and sorted

¾ cup dried black beans, rinsed and sorted

3 tablespoons cornmeal

Chopped fresh cilantro and feta cheese (optional)

1. Season pork with 1 teaspoon salt and 1 teaspoon black pepper. Heat oil in large skillet over medium-high heat. Cook pork in batches 6 minutes or until browned on all sides. Remove to **CROCK-POT**® slow cooker using slotted spoon.

2. Heat same skillet over medium heat. Add bacon; cook and stir until crisp. Remove to **CROCK-POT**® slow cooker using slotted spoon.

3. Pour off all but 2 tablespoons fat from skillet. Return skillet to medium heat. Add onions and bell pepper; cook and stir 6 minutes or just until softened. Stir in chili powder, tomato paste, garlic, cumin, paprika, remaining 2½ teaspoons salt and remaining ¼ teaspoon black pepper; cook and stir 1 minute. Stir in ale. Bring to a simmer, scraping up any browned bits from the bottom of skillet. Pour over pork in **CROCK-POT**® slow cooker. Stir in tomatoes, water, beans and cornmeal.

4. Cover; cook on LOW 10 hours. Turn off heat. Let stand 10 minutes. Skim off and discard fat. Top each serving with cilantro and cheese, if desired.

SPICY ITALIAN BEEF

MAKES 8 TO 10 SERVINGS

1 boneless beef
   chuck roast (3 to
   4 pounds)*

1 jar (12 ounces)
   pepperoncini
   peppers**

1 can (about
   14 ounces) beef
   broth

1 can (12 ounces) beer

1 onion, minced

2 tablespoons Italian
   seasoning

1 loaf French bread,
   cut into thick
   slices

8 to 10 slices
   provolone cheese
   (optional)

*Unless you have a 5-, 6- or 7-quart **CROCK-POT**® slow cooker, cut any roast larger than 2½ pounds in half so it cooks completely.

**Pepperoncini peppers are pickled peppers sold in jars with brine. They are available in the condiment aisle of large supermarkets.

1. Place roast in **CROCK-POT**® slow cooker.

2. Drain pepperoncini peppers. Pull off stem ends and discard. Add pepperoncini peppers, broth, beer, onion and Italian seasoning to **CROCK-POT**® slow cooker; do not stir. Cover; cook on LOW 8 to 10 hours.

3. Remove beef to large cutting board; shred with two forks. Return beef to cooking liquid; mix well. Serve on French bread. Top with cheese, if desired.

INDEX

METRIC CONVERSION CHART

VOLUME MEASUREMENTS (dry)

1/8 teaspoon = 0.5 mL
1/4 teaspoon = 1 mL
1/2 teaspoon = 2 mL
3/4 teaspoon = 4 mL
1 teaspoon = 5 mL
1 tablespoon = 15 mL
2 tablespoons = 30 mL
1/4 cup = 60 mL
1/3 cup = 75 mL
1/2 cup = 125 mL
2/3 cup = 150 mL
3/4 cup = 175 mL
1 cup = 250 mL
2 cups = 1 pint = 500 mL
3 cups = 750 mL
4 cups = 1 quart = 1 L

VOLUME MEASUREMENTS (fluid)

1 fluid ounce (2 tablespoons) = 30 mL
4 fluid ounces (1/2 cup) = 125 mL
8 fluid ounces (1 cup) = 250 mL
12 fluid ounces (1 1/2 cups) = 375 mL
16 fluid ounces (2 cups) = 500 mL

WEIGHTS (mass)

1/2 ounce = 15 g
1 ounce = 30 g
3 ounces = 90 g
4 ounces = 120 g
8 ounces = 225 g
10 ounces = 285 g
12 ounces = 360 g
16 ounces = 1 pound = 450 g

DIMENSIONS

1/16 inch = 2 mm
1/8 inch = 3 mm
1/4 inch = 6 mm
1/2 inch = 1.5 cm
3/4 inch = 2 cm
1 inch = 2.5 cm

OVEN TEMPERATURES

250°F = 120°C
275°F = 140°C
300°F = 150°C
325°F = 160°C
350°F = 180°C
375°F = 190°C
400°F = 200°C
425°F = 220°C
450°F = 230°C

BAKING PAN SIZES

Utensil	Size in Inches/Quarts	Metric Volume	Size in Centimeters
Baking or Cake Pan (square or rectangular)	8×8×2	2 L	20×20×5
	9×9×2	2.5 L	23×23×5
	12×8×2	3 L	30×20×5
	13×9×2	3.5 L	33×23×5
Loaf Pan	8×4×3	1.5 L	20×10×7
	9×5×3	2 L	23×13×7
Round Layer Cake Pan	8×1½	1.2 L	20×4
	9×1½	1.5 L	23×4
Pie Plate	8×1¼	750 mL	20×3
	9×1¼	1 L	23×3
Baking Dish or Casserole	1 quart	1 L	—
	1½ quart	1.5 L	—
	2 quart	2 L	—